CW00921302

Living & Working in
the Netherlands

Living & Working in the Netherlands

All you need to know for a long or short-term stay

PAT RUSH
2nd edition

How To Books

Published by How To Books Ltd,
3 Newtec Place, Magdalen Road,
Oxford OX4 1RE, United Kingdom.
Tel: (01865) 793806. Fax: (01865) 248780.
email: info@howtobooks.co.uk
http://www.howtobooks.co.uk

First edition 1996
Second edition 2001

British Library Cataloguing in Publication Data.
A catalogue record for this book is available from
the British Library.

Cover design by Shireen Nathoo Design
Cover image by PhotoDisc
Cartoons by Mike Flanagan

Produced for How To Books by Deer Park Productions
Typeset by Anneset, Weston-super-Mare, N Somerset
Printed and bound by Cromwell Press, Trowbridge, Wiltshire

NOTE: The material contained in this book is set out in good
faith for general guidance and no liability can be accepted
for loss or expense incurred as a result of relying in particular
circumstances on statements made in the book. Laws and
regulations are complex and liable to change, and readers should
check the current position with the relevant authorities before
making personal arrangements.

Contents

List of Illustrations

Preface

to the second edition

I would like to thank all those who helped me with the compilation of this book. Dozens of individuals and organisations offered information and advice, either in person, by post or by telephone.

I would like to extend special thanks to the Royal Dutch Embassy in London, and the British Embassy in The Hague, who both sent huge quantities of information. The ACCESS organisation in The Hague provided invaluable insights into the kinds of problems faced by visitors. And the book would not have been possible without Wil Weinreder's patient answering of question after question about every aspect of Dutch life.

It is universally agreed that everyday life in the Netherlands can be extremely complicated – not least for those who do not speak the language. What's more, regulations and the like can change with alarming rapidity (as many have done since the first edition of this book). But, if you make the effort to understand the system, the benefits will often more than justify the time put in.

I hope that this book will set you off in the right direction, and make your stay in the Netherlands as memorable as my own.

Pat Rush

9

Fig. 1. The 12 provinces of the Netherlands

1

Introducing the Netherlands

It's only a small country. With a total area of around 16,000 square miles, the Netherlands is just one-fifth the size of the United Kingdom. Bounded by Germany to the east, Belgium to the south, and sea to the north and west, it measures just over 100 miles from west to east, and around 200 miles from north to south. But its 15 million inhabitants make it one of the most densely populated countries in the world, with a population density twice that of the UK and over 20 times that of the US.

Nearly half of the country's whole population lives in the so-called *randstad* – a largely urban area that includes the cities of Amsterdam, Rotterdam and The Hague, as well as Utrecht and Haarlem.

The Netherlands is divided into twelve provinces: Drenthe, Flevoland, Friesland, Gelderland, Groningen, Limburg, North Brabant, North Holland, Overijssel, South Holland, Utrecht and Zeeland. Technically, 'Holland' refers only to the provinces of North and South Holland. If you are talking about the whole country, it should be called the Netherlands – although you will find that even Dutch people sometimes use the term Holland when they mean the country as a whole.

LAND OF WIND AND WATER

Any visitor to the Netherlands will be struck by the flatness of the landscape. Even gentle hills are rare, except in part of the south-east. And with over one-third of the country actually below sea level, dykes are essential to protect it from the sea.

The country is also crossed by three major rivers – the Rhine, the Maas and the Scheldt. So water is an ever-present threat, and evidence of this can be seen at every turn. The whole country is criss-crossed by a network of canals and drainage ditches, and even the famous windmills exist mainly to pump water rather than to grind corn.

Reclamation of land from the sea is also a never-ending process, resulting in a constant yet peaceful growth in the country's area. The draining of the former Zuiderzee (now IJsselmeer), begun after the First World War, has alone yielded millions of acres and led to the creation of a whole new province, known as Flevoland, in 1986.

HISTORY

Megalithic tombs provide evidence of settlement as far back as 3,000 BC. The Romans arrived around 55 BC. Maastricht (Mosa Trajectum) was one of their settlements. Nijmegen was one of many others. They dug many canals before they eventually departed in the fifth century AD.

The Netherlands came under the house of Burgundy during the 15th century, and under Holy Roman Emperor Charles V in 1515. But in 1568 they rebelled against his strongly Catholic son, Philip II of Spain. The war of independence lasted for the next 80 years, but it was followed by the Golden Age, marked by colonial expansion and the flourishing of both arts and sciences.

War with England followed during the 17th century. But in 1689 the English crown was offered to William of Orange and his wife Mary, daughter of the deposed English king James II. William of Orange became William III of Great Britain and Ireland, and remained king until his death in 1702.

Further wars with England and France followed, with the Netherlands eventually becoming a province of France. But after French domination ended in 1813, Prince William VI of Orange became the first king of the Netherlands, Willem (or William) I, in 1815 – marking the start of the hereditary monarchy that continues to this day.

Belgium and Luxembourg also came under the Dutch crown. But the Belgians would later set up their own Catholic state. And by the end of the century an independent Grand Duchy of Luxembourg had also been established.

The present Queen Beatrix came to the throne on the abdication of her mother, Juliana, in 1980.

POLITICAL STRUCTURE

The Netherlands is a hereditary and constitutional monarchy with a parliamentary system of government.

There are two houses of parliament. The Lower House *(Tweede Kamer)* is made up of 150 members, elected by universal suffrage. The 75 members of the Upper House *(Eerste Kamer)* are elected by the provincial assemblies and, like the British House of Lords, they cannot actually propose or change bills. They can only delay them.

Elections to the Lower House are based on a system of proportional representation, with the percentage of votes won by a party throughout the country deciding the percentage of seats they will receive. As there are many political parties, no single party obtains an overall majority in elections, so governments are formed by coalitions between two or more parties.

THE DUTCH ECONOMY

At the time of writing, the economy of the Netherlands is a healthy one, with low inflation and a strong guilder.

Rotterdam is the world's largest port. Amsterdam's Schiphol Airport is the third largest in Europe. With three major rivers also flowing across the Netherlands and into the world's busiest sea, the country has become a centre for transport and distribution – the gateway to Europe.

The economy has a solid industrial base as well as a large service sector. But the relatively small agricultural sector is also significant, as it produces sizeable surpluses for export and also provides the basis for the food-processing and packaging industry.

TOLERANCE AND CONSERVATISM

The Dutch have a worldwide reputation for open-mindedness, and a tradition of welcoming people of every religious or political persuasion.

During the 1960s and '70s, for instance, Amsterdam became a real hippy haven. A liberal attitude towards **possession** of small quantities of drugs for personal use continues to this day. Special coffeeshops openly offering cannabis for sale remain a lasting image for many visitors.

But anyone who stays longer soon discovers that the famous tolerance goes hand in hand with a strong conservatism.

The work ethic is strong. The atmosphere in most offices may seem informal, and the clothing deceptively casual. But that doesn't mean that they have a casual approach to the job in hand. Getting the job done is what matters most, and that can mean long working days with the shortest of breaks.

The family, too, is very important, with special events like birthdays and weddings providing excuses for major family gatherings.

Getting to know people may seem hard at first. The Dutch directness can be disconcerting. And although superficial exchanges may seem friendly enough, it can take a long time to forge any closer contact. There's no point trying to rush things. With patience, close and enduring friendships can be made.

CASE STUDIES

Susan continues nursing

I'd visited the Netherlands many times and decided I would like to live here, at least for a while. I met Karel, a builder, soon after I arrived and we started living together about a year later. Now I've a job I enjoy at a major teaching hospital, and I couldn't imagine living anywhere else.

Ian takes a year or two off

I decided to take a year or two out after leaving college, before finding a regular job. I'd heard from fellow Scots about the good times they'd had in Holland, and decided I'd give it a try. I thought I could always earn a living busking on the streets of Amsterdam, even if I couldn't find a regular job.

Kay and Jonathan are transferred

We came here from the US five years ago, when Jonathan's company transferred him to their Rotterdam office. His work is very specialised, and they were keen to have him here. But we've two young children, aged four and seven. So we did make sure that there was a suitable school for them within easy reach. Although we expect to be here for some time, we don't expect to stay forever, and obviously didn't want their education to suffer.

Diane gets married – and divorced

I was married to a Dutchman for 14 years. We were divorced six years ago, but I stayed here so that my children (aged 17 and 19) could finish their education. I'm not sure what I will do then. I haven't found it easy to find work here. I do occasional freelance work for a publishing company, but it's not enough to live on, so I've had to find my way around the Dutch social security system.

2

Making the Move

TAKING THE FIRST STEPS

Even a very small amount of advance planning can save a huge amount of time, energy and frustration on your arrival in the Netherlands. So if you can, do take the time to read all of this book before you go. There are certain steps that must be taken before you leave. Failure to complete the necessary formalities could result in your being denied entry to the Netherlands. Or you could find yourself being forced to leave the country prematurely.

In particular, you should be sure to read the section on Dealing with Customs (page 19) and the chapter on Completing the Formalities, especially if you come from a non-EU country. If you need a visa to enter the country, you will need to obtain it before departure. And some foreign nationals planning to work in the Netherlands must also apply for a temporary residence permit **before setting off**.

You will also need to organise some kind of **health insurance**, to cover you until you become part of the Dutch system. And if you are drawing any kind of benefit in your home country, you will generally need to make arrangements for any continuing payments before you leave (see page 84).

Gathering essential documents

As you will learn from later sections in this book, you will need to present various documents either on entry to the country or when completing the formalities after your arrival. Make sure that you have the following with you:

● a valid passport (including visa if necessary)

● your Temporary Residence Permit, if you need one

● any contract or correspondence with your future employer, if you have one

15

- your address in the Netherlands

- your birth certificate (a British birth certificate will need to be legalised – see page 28)

- all papers relating to any present or previous marriage, including any divorce or death certificates

- your health insurance documents

- sufficient funds to last until you receive your first salary, or to pay for a return ticket should you decide to return home.

Smoothing your way

There are a number of other things you could do to help make things easier on arrival:

- Find out as much about the country as you can (you'll find plenty of sources of information in this book).

- Learn as much Dutch as you can in the time you have. Not only will it make life easier, it will also improve your work prospects if you do not yet have a job (see page 55).

- Obtain a supply of colour passport-type photographs. You will find that you are constantly being asked for them – by official departments and prospective employers, for instance. In addition, some officials will not accept photographs taken in automatic booths, so you will need to have some taken by a photographer.

- Ask your most recent employer(s) for a testimonial that you can show to prospective employers in the Netherlands.

- Find some people who would be willing to provide references (including personal references) for potential employers.

- Take out a comprehensive travel insurance policy that covers not only health but also luggage, accidents and personal liability. It will provide peace of mind both when you are travelling and after arrival.

ORGANISING THE MOVE

If you are planning to travel with just a few suitcases, you will probably simply take them with you. But if you have a whole household to pack up and transport to the Netherlands, **professional removers** can make things a good deal easier.

Hiring a van and doing all the work yourself could be another possibility if the distance is not too great. But savings could be minimal or non-existent by the time you have arranged for the return of the van. And you will also have to deal with all the paperwork yourself.

Finding a removal company

There is, in general, free movement of goods within the EU. So if you are travelling from Britain to the Netherlands the procedure is similar to that for a move within Britain itself. The British Association of Removers can send you details of members, and also has some leaflets containing general hints for those moving house.

- British Association of Removers, 3 Churchill Court, 58 Station Road, North Harrow HA2 7SA, UK. Tel: (020) 8861 3331. Fax (020) 8861 3332.

Ask for estimates from two or three different removal companies, both large and small, and then check the quotes carefully to see exactly what is covered.

You may, for instance, think that it is cheaper – and perhaps even safer – to pack your belongings yourself. But a professional remover will be much more experienced at it than you are, and the additional cost may be minimal. In addition, the **insurance** available from your remover will not cover items packed by others, so it could be a false economy.

You should, in any case, check the amount of insurance cover that is provided. If it is not enough to cover everything you will be taking, you will need to take out extra cover – and take this into account when comparing costs.

If you need to put items into **storage** – either until your return, or until you have found somewhere permanent to live – these costs will also have to be taken into account.

Shipping your belongings

If you are travelling from outside Europe, you may be offered a choice between several different forms of shipping for your belongings. There are advantages and disadvantages to each.

With a **full container load**, for instance, your belongings have a container to themselves. If you don't have sufficient to fill a container, however, they can be sent **groupage**, with the remaining space occupied by goods belonging to someone else. The drawback is that you could find yourself waiting a considerable time before the remover finds someone wishing to make use of the remaining space. So ask for an estimated shipping time.

If you have less than a container load, therefore, you may wish to consider using **direct steamer services**, with your belongings packed into a sturdy case. This is more expensive than groupage, but can be much faster.

Deciding what to ship

In general it is cheaper to take most things with you than to pay for the costs of replacements. But a thorough clear out is obviously doubly important when your move is to another country. You may also find that Dutch houses, and their kitchens, are smaller than those you are used to – another good reason to be ruthless about discarding things you don't need.

Removal costs are generally based on **volume** rather than weight. So this must be borne in mind when making your decisions, too. Books, for instance, may be heavy, but a large number can be packed into a relatively small space. As replacements will often be difficult to find, and could also be very expensive, it may well be worth your while to take them with you.

You will also need to check out the suitability of any electrical equipment that you wish to take with you. You don't want to pay for transport of a bulky item only to find it won't work when you get it there. Consider, too, whether spare parts will be available if the item breaks down. And if you need an adaptor, it may be easier to buy it before you go (see page 65).

Packing

If the packing is to be done by the removal company, they will make an inventory for you. Otherwise you will have to make it yourself.

Your removers will also be able to advise you on what not to pack. But you will need to be especially vigilant about **flammable substances**. Heat can build up enormously inside a crate, and even a seemingly innocuous cleaning product could lead to an explosion or a fire which, at the very least, would ruin your other possessions.

Liquids can also cause enormous damage. If you must take some with you, make sure that any containers are sealed securely with tape, and then seal them inside individual polythene bags.

Tying up loose ends

Arranging for the reading of meters and disconnection of services is part of every house move. So, too, is informing people of your new address, arranging for mail to be forwarded, cancelling deliveries of milk and newspapers, and returning library books and suchlike.

But if you are moving to another country – whether temporarily or indefinitely – you need to deal with numerous other loose ends. You don't want to pay unnecessarily for services you no longer use. And you don't want to find unexpected bills following you, or awaiting your eventual return.

Taxes and Social Security
You will need to contact Income Tax, Social Security and Motor Tax offices, *etc,* to tell them of your plans.

Money
You will need to close credit accounts that are no longer of use, and decide what is to be done about any bank accounts, credit cards and so on. Outstanding hire purchase payments will need to be made, and any rental agreements cancelled.

Social
Membership of certain book clubs and record clubs may no longer be possible. You may also want to resign from other clubs which are no longer of any benefit to you. Or you may be able to arrange non-residential status at a lower fee. And magazine subscriptions may have to be cancelled, or changed to incorporate higher postal charges.

Health
If you need prescriptions to tide you over the period of the move, you'll need to get these filled before you leave. It would also be useful to find out the generic names for any medicines that you use, to give to your doctor or pharmacist in the Netherlands.

Schools
Obtain copies of your children's school and medical records to pass on to their school in the Netherlands.

General
Make sure that your address book is totally up to date. You may be used to looking up that friend's number in the phone book, or ringing her to check on the postcode every time you want to send a Christmas card. But it won't be so easy when you are in another country.

DEALING WITH CUSTOMS

Importing household effects
If you are resident in an EU country, you will not be required to pay import duty on any household effects you import into the Netherlands.

Residents of non-EU countries can also apply for exemption of import duties on personal effects, subject to certain conditions. But you must apply **in advance** to the Customs office which has jurisdiction over your future place of residence.

Details will be found in the booklet *Moving to the Netherlands* published by the Customs Directorate (*Directie douane*) in Rotterdam.

- Tax and Customs Administration, Customs Directorate (*Directie Douane*), Postbus 50964, 3007 BG Rotterdam, The Netherlands. Tel. (010) 290 4949.

The booklet includes the addresses, telephone and fax numbers for the various regional Customs offices.

If you are moving from a non-EU country, you will also need to declare the imported goods to the Customs authorities whether or not you have a permit to import them free of tax. For this purpose, you must apply in advance for a special form known as a Single Administrative Document.

The regional Customs offices will be able to answer specific enquiries. But there is also a national help line for general customs enquiries. The number is (045) 574 3031 and the service operates from 8.00 to 22.00, local time, Monday to Thursday, and 8.00 to 17.00 on Fridays.

Importing cars and motor cycles

If you want to import a car or motor cycle into the Netherlands tax free, you must apply in advance, even if you are importing the car from a country in the EU. Although there is no import duty on goods imported from the EU, and the VAT (*BTW*) has already been paid, you would be liable for Car and Motor Cycle Tax (*BPM*) if you did not apply for exemption.

Applications should be made to the Customs district for the area you will be living in. As mentioned above, their addresses can be found in the booklet *Moving to the Netherlands,* obtainable from the Dutch Customs Directorate. If you are not sure which area you will be in, you should ring the national Customs help line on (045) 574 3031 for assistance.

Certain conditions must be met in order to qualify for tax exemption. You must, for instance, have been in possession of the vehicle for at least six months. It must have been in use in the country you are now leaving. And you will not be able to lend it out, pledge, lease or sell it for 12 months after your arrival in the Netherlands without becoming liable for tax on it.

If you are moving from a non-EU country, you will also need to declare the car on the Single Administrative Document mentioned above.

Registering your vehicle

Before you can drive your car or motor cycle in the Netherlands you will need to get a Dutch vehicle registration certificate. But before it can be issued a **technical inspection** of the vehicle must be carried out by the National Vehicle Administration Agency (*Rijksdienst voor het Wegverkeer,* or *RDW*).

● RDW Centrum voor voortuigtechniek en informatie, Bureau inlichtingen en correspondentie, Skager Rak 10, 9642 CZ Veendam, The Netherlands. Tel: (0598) 62 42 40.

When your vehicle is inspected you will be given a Motor Vehicle Tax (*BPM*) declaration form, on which you can request exemption from Motor Vehicle Tax. Several copies of this must then be sent to one of the customs offices at which *BPM* declarations can be lodged. Again, addresses will be found in the booklet *Moving to the Netherlands*.

A vehicle registration certificate will then be sent to you. But you will need to obtain your own registration plates, at a recognised garage.

You should have your vehicle inspected, and send off your *BPM* declaration, as soon as possible after your arrival.

Paying road tax

As soon as your car or motor cycle is registered, you will have to start paying road tax. The transfer of your name to the vehicle registration certificate actually acts as a road tax declaration. You will therefore automatically receive a giro payment slip from the Tax Administration (*Belastingdienst*) soon afterwards. The Tax Administration office will also answer any queries you may have on motor vehicle tax.

● Belastingdienst/Centraal bureau motorrijtuigenbelasting, Postbus 9047, 7300 GJ Apeldoorn, The Netherlands. Tel: (055) 578 2244.

Insuring your vehicle

By law, you must have at least **third party insurance** for your vehicle.

Taking your pets with you

If you want to take a cat or dog with you to the Netherlands from the United Kingdom or Ireland, you will need to accompany your pet yourself and you will need a health certificate for it. This must be collected from an authorised veterinarian no more than ten days before your departure.

The rabies vaccination once required for The Netherlands is no longer needed, but the certificate should state that the animal is healthy. It should also include the name of the owner and a description of the pet (breed, age and sex, as well as colour and type of coat and any markings).

Pitbull terriers and some other breeds are not allowed to enter the country, and there are special rules for dogs and cats imported for commercial purposes and not as pets.

If you later return to Britain with your pet you will, of course, have to satisfy whatever regulations are then in force. So you will need to bear this in mind – especially if your stay is to be a limited one. Up-to-date information can be obtained from the Ministry of Agriculture, which has a special pets helpline.

- Ministry of Agriculture, Fisheries and Food, 1a Page Street, London SW1P 4PQ, UK. Tel: (0870) 241 1710.

Paying dog tax

You won't need a dog licence in the Netherlands, but you will need to pay dog tax (*hondenbelasting*) at the Town Hall *(Stadhuis)*. You will need to pay for each dog, if you have more than one.

CASE STUDIES

Susan organises her own move

I'd always planned to stay here for quite a while, as I'd visited the country many times and fallen in love with it. But I didn't have a great many belongings – no furniture or anything. A friend hired a van in the end, and brought me over on the ferry one weekend. As I'm from another EU country, I didn't need any special papers for Customs.

Ian muddles through

I don't know how long I'll be staying, so I came here with just a couple of suitcases and my guitar. But life would have been much easier if I'd done a little advance planning. I didn't realise I'd need things like my birth certificate, and I had to get my parents to help me out on more than one occasion. It's not nearly so easy to do things from a distance.

Kay and Jonathan call in the experts

We were lucky because Jonathan's company were paying for all our removal costs and also suggested a removal company that they had used many times before. So we were able to leave most of the actual moving organisation to them. They offered lots of advice about things we hadn't even thought of, and really made the transition easy.

Diane looks back

I never really intended to stay in the Netherlands. I came for a short visit and met my husband shortly before I was due to leave. So it took me years to get my belongings over here. I'd bring a few things back every time I went to visit my family and then finally, after about ten years, I decided that what was left couldn't be very important. So my parents gave the last few boxes away.

CHECKLIST

1.   Have you thought about what you need to do before you leave?

2.   What are you going to take with you?

3.   What will be the best way for you to ship your belongings?

3

Completing the Formalities

Since regulations regarding immigration procedures are extremely complicated and constantly liable to change, it is essential to obtain the most up-to-date information possible **before you leave**. What follows is merely a guide, based on information available at the time of writing. To confirm that these regulations still apply or to enquire about individual circumstances, you should contact the Dutch embassy in your own country, and/or your own country's embassy in the Netherlands itself. (Some addresses are given in the Useful Addresses section.)

A booklet entitled *Working in the Netherlands,* for instance, is available from the Dutch embassy in London and includes a section on immigration and registration.

- Royal Netherlands Embassy, 38 Hyde Park Gate, London SW7 5DP, UK. Tel: (020) 590 3200.

The British Embassy in The Hague also publishes a booklet on *Living and Working in the Netherlands,* and their very informative website includes answers to many frequently asked questions.

- British Embassy, Lange Voorhout 10, 2514 ED The Hague, The Netherlands. Tel: (070) 4270 427. Website: http://www.britain.nl

The American Consulate General in Amsterdam also produces a *General Information Guide for American Citizens Residing in the Kingdom of the Netherlands.*

- American Consulate General, Museumplein 19, 1071 DJ Amsterdam, The Netherlands. Tel: (020) 575 5309.

In addition, a number of booklets and factsheets on Dutch immigration policy, in English, are available from the Ministry of Justice.

- Ministerie van Justitie, Immigration and Naturalization Service,

Postbus 30125, 2500 GC Den Haag, The Netherlands. Tel: (070) 370 3124/3144. Fax: (070) 370 3134.

ENTERING THE NETHERLANDS

If you are intending to live in the Netherlands you must, of course, have a **valid passport** for every member of your family who will be moving with you. If you are a British national, you will need a full UK or EU passport.

British nationals (and those from other **EU countries**) do not need work permits before taking up employment in the Netherlands. You are free to enter the country for up to three months in order to look for work or to set up a business there. But you may still be asked to provide evidence that you have sufficient funds for your stay and that the cost of your return journey is secured.

Regulations for those from **non-EU countries** are more complex. Further information is contained in the following sections. But you should be sure to contact a Netherlands diplomatic or consular representative in your own country before you leave, to make sure that you have all the documents required. Otherwise, you could find yourself on the next plane back.

APPLYING FOR A VISA

Citizens of EU countries do not need visas to enter the Netherlands. If you are travelling from a non-EU country, however, a visa may be required. If this is the case, you will need to obtain it before you set off. The Netherlands embassy in your country of residence will be able to give you further information.

US citizens do not need visas, for instance, nor do those from Australia. If you are from a country that does, it is vital that you obtain the correct visa for your needs. If you have the wrong kind, you will face enormous, and perhaps insurmountable, problems when you try to change it.

OBTAINING A RESIDENCE PERMIT

EU citizens do not have to apply for a **residence permit**, but difficulties can arise if you do not have one. Banks, telephone or health insurance companies may all want to see your residence document before entering into any contract with you. Some employers, too, may want to see it.

Those who are not from EU or EEA (European Economic Area) countries, on the other hand, must obtain a residence permit if they intend to stay in the Netherlands for longer than three months, or to take up employment there. Even if you do not need a work permit, you do need permission to reside in the Netherlands.

Residence permits are obtained from the Aliens Police (*Vreemdelingenpolitie*). In most of the larger cities, you will find them at the local police headquarters. But in smaller communities they have their offices in or near the Town Hall *(Stadhuis)*. The exception is Amsterdam, where they can be found at Johan Huizingalaan 757, 1066 VH Amsterdam, The Netherlands. Tel: (020) 559 6300.

What to do if you are from the EU

Taking the first steps

It is advisable to apply to the Aliens Police as soon as possible after your arrival. All you will need at this stage is a passport, preferably one that is valid for the length of your stay. You will generally then be granted a residence permit for three months.

During that time you will need to do the following and take the necessary documentation with you when you visit the Police again:

- Obtain evidence of employment, or of some other means of subsistence.

- Take out health insurance of some kind.

- Add your name to the **Population Register** (*Bevolkingsregister*, see below).

- Obtain a social security/tax number(*SOFI nummer*) from your local tax office (*Belastingkantoor*, see below).

Obtaining the residence permit

If you are in acceptable and permanent employment, and have fulfilled all the other requirements, you may be given a permit for a further five years, on payment of the relevant stamp duty charge.

If, however, your work is temporary or casual, you will probably only be given a residence permit to cover the period involved. You will have to apply for another permit before it expires. Also, if you are planning to become self employed, you will still need a residence permit, but will need to produce additional documents. You will be referred to the Immigration and Naturalization Department of the Ministry of Justice in The Hague.

What to do if you are not an EU citizen

You may need to acquire a temporary residence permit (*Machtiging voor Voorlopig Verblijf*) before you leave. So it is essential that you first contact the Netherlands embassy in the country where you are now living. If you need a temporary permit and travel to the Netherlands without one, you will not be able to stay. You cannot obtain the necessary permit after your arrival. Once in the Netherlands you will need to report to the Aliens Police within three days.

At the time of writing, residents of the US, Canada, Australia and New Zealand are among those who do not need temporary residence permits before travelling. They are free to visit the Netherlands for three months, but will need to report to the Aliens Police if they intend to stay for longer. As with EU citizens, it may be beneficial to do this sooner rather than later.

Various conditions will have to be met before a residence permit (usually for no more than one year at first) can be granted, and a **fee will be charged** whether or not the permit is granted.

You will have to provide evidence that you are able to support yourself during your stay, and that you have acquired medical insurance.

Finding out more

A special anonymous helpline has been set up by the Aliens Police in The Hague to help those requiring further information. You can telephone them on (070) 360 9879 between 8.00 and 16.00 on weekdays.

A few tips that may help

- Visits to the Aliens Police can be time-consuming, with long queues, especially in major cities. Phone up in advance to find out the office's opening times, and then get there early. Otherwise you run the risk of having to return the next day because the office closed before you reached the front of the queue.

- Even if not specifically requested, always take as many papers as possible with you: passports, birth certificates (including that of any children), marriage/divorce papers, work contracts, correspondence with prospective employers, your temporary residence permit if you have one, and anything else which you feel may be relevant. And don't forget details of your address in the Netherlands.

- Always have a supply of passport-sized photos with you (and not from automatic machines).

- When you return for your long-term permit, make sure you also take with you evidence of your registration with the Population Register and Tax Office and of taking out health insurance (page 28).

ADDING YOUR NAME TO THE POPULATION REGISTER

Every resident of the Netherlands (including Dutch citizens) must register with the Population Register *(Bevolkingsregister)* at the Town Hall *(Stadhuis)*. This should be done after your initial visit to the Aliens Police.
    You should take with you:

- passport

- birth certificate

- marriage certificate

- divorce or death certificates relating to any previous marriages

- evidence of your marital or civil status.

Since the UK does not have a population register, a declaration of your marital or civil status, made before a consular official at the British Consulate General in Amsterdam, will be accepted by the Dutch authorities.

- British Consulate General, Koningslaan 44, 1075 AE Amsterdam, The Netherlands. Tel: (020) 676 4343. Fax: (020) 676 1069.

British certificates may have to be legalised by the Foreign and Commonwealth Office (FCO) by means of an 'apostille', to confirm the authenticity of the document and the signatory. To do this, send the relevant document by registered post to the Legalisation Office at the FCO.

- The Legalisation Office, Foreign and Commonwealth Office, 20 Victoria Street, London SW1H 0NZ, UK. Tel: (020) 7210 2521. Fax: (020) 7210 2526.

There is a fee for this service (telephone for details). This should accompany the documents, which will be returned within about a week.
    When registering with the *Bevolkingsregister,* you may be asked for the full names and the dates and places of birth of your parents. So if you don't have these details, you will need to find them before visiting the Town Hall. And you will also need proof of where you are living, such as a rent contract if you have one.

OBTAINING A FISCAL SOCIAL NUMBER

You should also obtain a social security tax number (known in the

Netherlands as a *SOFI nummer*) from your local Tax Office
(Belastingkantoor). This should be done after you register with the
Bevolkingsregister. If you are in employment, however, your employer will
complete the necessary formalities for you.

If you are making the application yourself, you should make sure you
have your UK National Insurance number with you, if you have one.

APPLYING FOR WORK PERMITS

If you are from a country outside the European Union and plan to work in
the Netherlands, you will need a **work permit** (*werkvergunning* or
terwerkstellingsvergunning). This is true whether you are employed as a
shop assistant in your local grocery store or as the managing director of a
giant corporation.

Permits are issued by the Ministry of Social Affairs and Labour
(*Ministerie van Sociale Zaken en Werkgelegenheid*). Information about
work permits can be obtained from your Regional Employment Office
(*Gewestelijk Arbeidsbureau*). The application process will take between
one and three months to complete.

In general, work permits are only issued to people with special skills that
are unavailable in the Netherlands. So those from outside the EU are
always advised to obtain further information before travelling. If you are
already in the Netherlands, however, seek as much advice as you can from
others who have been in the same situation.

If, on the other hand, you find work with a major company that regularly
recruits staff from outside the EU, you may find that many of the
formalities are dealt with by your employer – possibly even before you
arrive in the country.

ARRANGING HEALTH INSURANCE

Before you get your residence permit, you will also need to have some kind
of health insurance. Either you will be covered by a local *ziekenfonds,*
which is a state-controlled insurance, or you will need to take out a policy
with a private company. If your annual income is below a certain level, you
will generally be insured with the *ziekenfonds* through your employer
unless you are self-employed. (For further information, see Chapter 8.)

TAKING IT STEP BY STEP

EU citizens

1. Make sure you have copies of your birth certificate, any marriage cer-
    tificate, and any separation, divorce or death certificates relating to

your present or previous marriage(s). You will also need a number of colour passport photos (not from automatic machines).

2. If you are British, have your documents legalised by the Foreign and Commonwealth Office.

3. Register with the Aliens Police as soon as possible after your arrival.

4. Register with the Population Register.

5. Obtain a *SOFI* number.

6. Once employment is finalised and health insurance is obtained, return to the Aliens Police with all the documentation, to apply for a five-year residence permit.

Non-EU citizens

Additional steps may include applying for a temporary residence permit before you leave, and acquiring a work permit. You may also be required to report to the Aliens Police at certain intervals while your request for a residence permit is processed.

You should ask the Netherlands diplomatic or consular representative in your country of residence what procedure you should follow before leaving. In the Netherlands itself, your own country's consular representative should be able to supply further information. But it is also worth talking to other expatriates about their experiences, especially if they are recent arrivals. Sometimes procedures change, and you may be able to save both time and frustration if you know in advance what is required of you.

CASE STUDIES

Susan plans ahead

I obtained a lot of information from the Dutch Embassy in London before I left, so I knew it was advisable to apply for a residence permit and that I would have to register at the Town Hall and so on. But I still found that I kept turning up somewhere without all the information or papers I needed. It would have helped if I'd known some more expatriates, I think. Then I could have learnt from their mistakes.

Ian's friends show him the way

I met up with a load of other Scots in Amsterdam almost as soon as I arrived, and they told me how to go about getting the necessary paperwork completed. I felt really sorry for other people who waited for hours to get to the front of the queue, only to be turned away because they hadn't brought any passport photos with them. Some people find themselves going back two or three times because they've forgotten some vital document or piece of information. So it really does pay to ask around.

Jonathan's company helps out

My personnel department took care of many of the initial formalities, which saved us a lot of the frustration experienced by some of our new friends here. It's not easy for those from outside the EU to get work permits. But my work is very specialised, and my company employs quite a lot of Americans, so they knew all the procedures to follow.

Diane looks back

Because I wasn't intending to stay here, I didn't have any of the papers I needed for the Population Register and so on. But I went back to England for a weekend to pick up everything I needed. I'd already been to the Aliens Police and knew what they wanted to see. And my husband-to-be, being Dutch, made some other helpful suggestions.

CHECKLIST

1. Do you have all the documents you need?

2. Do you know the order in which you must deal with the formalities?

3. Do you know anyone who has gone through the procedure recently and could give you some useful tips?

4

Finding Your Way Around

The public transport system in the Netherlands is one of the best in the world. The Dutch are all too aware of the damage caused to the environment by the excessive use of private cars. So there has been a conscious attempt to entice people to make greater use of buses, trams and trains. The result is a well-integrated system with many cost-cutting tickets for frequent users.

Information on all forms of public transport can be obtained by ringing 0900-9292 (a premium-rate line). They will even tell you how to get from a given address to another.

TRAVELLING ON BUSES, TRAMS AND METRO

For travel on buses, trams and, in Amsterdam and Rotterdam, the metro, you will normally need to buy a ticket known as a *strippenkaart*, which is made up of a number of individual strips, or *strippen*. The more strips you buy at once, the cheaper your travel becomes.

Small tickets made up of two, three or eight strips can be bought from the driver as you board the tram or bus. But it is much more economical to buy tickets of 15 or 45 strips, which are available from bus stations, post offices and some tobacconists, bookshops and supermarkets. The larger ticket has strips on both sides, so remember to turn it over and use the other side.

There are reduced-price tickets for children aged between four and twelve, and also for those over 65 who hold a 65+ pass. The same tickets can also be used for larger dogs. (Small dogs which can be carried in a bag or basket can travel free.)

For details of other tickets, ask your local transport office for the multi-language brochure, or write to Postbus 55, 2501 CB Den Haag, The Netherlands.

It is important to remember, however, that you **must validate** your ticket at the start of every journey. If you buy your ticket from the driver, he will normally stamp it for you. But if you buy your ticket in advance, it must be stamped at the start of your journey. Otherwise it is not valid, and

Number of strips cancelled	Number of zones in which you may travel	Time for which your ticket is valid (in hrs)
2	1	1
3	2	1
4	3	1
5	4	1.5
6	5	1.5
7	6	1.5
8	7	2
9	8	2
10	9	2
11	10	3
12	11	3
13	12	3
14	13	3
15	14	3
16	15	3
17	16	3.5
18	17	3.5
19	18	3.5

Fig. 2. Validity of stamped *strippenkaarten*.

you could be liable to pay a spot fine equal to many times the fare that was due.

Choosing the correct number of strips

For public transport purposes, the whole country is divided into **zones** of about 4.5 km across. Basically, the number of strips you require for a journey is equal to the number of zones you will be passing through plus one. So if all your journey is in a single zone, you will need two strips. But a journey that takes you into three zones needs four strips.

If you don't know how many zones you will be passing through, you may find a map or diagram at the bus or tram stop. If not, simply tell the driver or conductor your destination, or write it down to show him if that is easier.

In Amsterdam, transport information offices should be able to give you a map of the complete public transport system.

Stamping the ticket

The strips are numbered on the left-hand-side. But you don't have to stamp every single one. If you need four strips for your first journey and six strips for your second, you will stamp strip 4 at the start of your first trip and strip 10 (4+6) at the start of the second.

To stamp the fourth strip, fold your ticket above strip 4, and hold it with strip 4 facing *upwards*. Then insert the folded edge into the slot in the ticket-stamping machine. You'll hear the machine stamp the ticket with some numbers followed by the date and the time.

You will find yellow stamping machines at the rear of trams. On Amsterdam light rail trains they are near doors and in the Metro you will find them near the stairs to the platforms. On most buses, you have to ask the driver to stamp your ticket.

Validity of stamped tickets

The date and time stamps are important: once your ticket is stamped for the required number of zones, you can change to other buses, trams or metro trains within those zones as often as you like, provided that you don't exceed the time limit allowed.

For instance, if you have stamped two to four strips (covering one to three zones), you can change as many times as you like for a whole hour, provided you stay within those zones. Stamping 17 to 19 strips (for 16 or more zones) allows you 3.5 hours.

Figure 2 shows the time limits for two to 19 strips. As long as you make your last change within that time, and stay within the relevant number of zones, your ticket remains valid. If your time runs out before you make your last change, however, you will have to re-stamp your ticket to cover the number of zones still left to travel.

Buying tickets for regular journeys

For regular journeys, such as those to work and school, it may be worth buying a weekly, monthly or annual season ticket or *abonnement*. These are on sale at transport offices and, in many cases, at post offices and other outlets. Such tickets allow travel within a certain number of zones which is dependent on the so-called star value (*sterwaarde*) of the ticket.

The number of a central zone will be printed on the ticket. A one-star ticket allows travel only in that central zone. But with a two-star ticket you can travel in the central zone and any zone adjacent to it, in any direction. A three-star ticket allows you to travel in the central zone and the first two neighbouring zones in any direction. Similarly, there are four-, five- and six-star tickets, and tickets allowing travel throughout the Netherlands.

Season tickets are thus valid for given areas rather than over specific routes, and this can have some interesting consequences, as Figure 3 shows.

You will need an identity card (*stamkaart*) to go with your ticket, so make sure you take a recent photo with you the first time you buy one. The identity card will be valid for five years. You must write its number in ink on every season ticket you buy, in the space marked *stamkaart nummer invullen*.

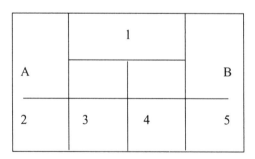

A trip from A to B will take you through four zones. If you choose Zone 3 or Zone 4 as your central zone, you will need a three-star ticket for the journey. But if you choose Zone 1 as your central zone, you will only need a two-star ticket, as each zone you are travelling in is adjacent to your central zone.

Fig. 3. Travelling through four zones with a two-star ticket.

Alighting from buses and trams

You must alert the driver if you want to get off a bus or tram. Otherwise, even if he stops to pick up passengers, he may not release the exit doors. You'll usually find buttons for this purpose (marked *stop*) on the sides of the vehicle. If the doors still don't open when the vehicle stops, look for a button marked *deur open* and press it to open the door.

Metro trains stop at every station. But again you will need to press the button marked *deur open* in order to open the doors.

On trams, you will find that the doors close automatically after a short time. To prevent them doing this, keep a foot on the bottom step (if you want to hold the doors open for a friend, for instance).

TRAVELLING BY TRAIN

Travel by train within the Netherlands is easy and the service is efficient. You'll find that staff are helpful and most speak at least a little English. So if you have any problems, all you have to do is ask.

Basically, though, all you have to do is buy your ticket – either at the ticket office or from a ticket machine – and board the train. And again there are spot fines for those caught without a ticket.

Using the ticket machine

There are machines at every station, selling a wide range of tickets to every destination in the country. Simply look at the list and then use the pad to the right to key in the relevant code for the town.

Under the keypad you will find buttons which can be used to choose the type of ticket you require: first or second class (*1e/2e klas*); without or with discount (*vol tarief/korting*); valid same day or without date (*alleen vandaag geldig/zonder datum* – see below). You can also indicate whether you want a single (*enkele reis*), day return (*dagretour*), five-return ticket (*5-retourkaart*), evening return (*avondretour*, for which you need a special discount card, or *voordeelsurenkaart*), or weekend return (*weekend retour*).

Once you've made your choice, the window on the top right of the machine will show the amount payable and whether you must insert the exact money (*Hoeft niet gepast* = exact money not necessary). Arrows under this window will flash to indicate that payment can be made by inserting coins in the slot to the left or your *PIN-pas* (see page 48) in the slot to the right.

After a few seconds you can take your ticket and any change or, if you requested one, your *PIN* payment slip from the slot in the bottom left of the machine.

If the machine is not working and you cannot buy your ticket from another machine or a ticket office, tell the conductor on the train as soon as you board. He will then know that you are not trying to evade payment.

Undated tickets must be stamped in a machine or at the ticket office before you start your journey.

Choosing your rail ticket

Many different kinds of ticket are available. It would be impossible to list them all – and, in any case, they are constantly changing. So the information given here should be taken as just a guideline to the kinds of tickets you should be able to buy. You can obtain more detailed information at any station. It's useful to know, though, that some English-language brochures are intended more for tourists than residents. So they may not mention all the possibilities.

At the time of writing, single (*enkele reis*) and day return (*dagretour*) tickets are valid for use on the date given, and up to 4.00 am the following morning. A weekend return (*weekend retour*) can be used if both outward and return journeys take place between 7.00 pm on Friday evening and 4.00 am on the following Monday morning. There is also a five-return ticket (*5-retourkaart*), valid for five return journeys to and from the same destination. (You will need to get it stamped in a machine or at the ticket office before starting each journey.)

A one-day Rover ticket (*dagkaart*) offers unlimited travel throughout the Netherlands on the date specified.

Buying tickets for regular journeys

Again, various season tickets (*abonnementen*) are available for regular journeys, like those to and from work.

A monthly *maandtrajectkaart*, for instance, can be used to travel over a given route for a whole month. It can also be combined with a one-, two- or three-zone Public Transport Link ticket (*stad-streekabonnement*) for bus, tram and metro.

Similarly, an annual *jaartrajectkaart* can be used for travel over a given route for a whole year, and can again be combined with a Public Transport Link ticket for buses, trams and metro, covering up to three zones. In addition, it gives reductions on other train tickets outside peak hours, in the so-called *voordeeluren*, or bargain hours.

A *maandnetkaart*, on the other hand, gives a month's unlimited travel on all trains throughout the Netherlands. This, too, can be combined with a Public Transport Link ticket (*stad-streekabonnement*) allowing unlimited travel by bus, tram and metro.

There are also annual tickets for unlimited travel on all trains throughout the Netherlands (*NS-jaarkaart*) or all trains, buses, trams and metros (*OV-jaarkaart*). In these cases, additional tickets can be purchased at relatively little cost for certain others living with you. But you'll need a copy of the relevant entry in the Population Register (*een uittreksel uit het Bevolkingsregister*).

Travelling with children

Children aged three and under travel free if they do not take up an additional seat. For children aged between four and 11, a reduced fare is payable. But for those accompanied by a fare-paying adult aged 19 years or more, a flat-rate *Railrunner* ticket can be bought for a nominal charge. This covers the child for the same journey as the adult. Up to three children can travel on *Railrunner* tickets with each adult.

Children of 12 and over pay the adult fare. But monthly season tickets are available at reduced rates for daily travel to and from school.

Travelling outside peak times

If you regularly travel outside the peak hours (*ie*, at weekends, or after 9.00 am during the week), you could also benefit from buying one of the annual off-peak tickets (*voordeelurenkaarten*). There are extra advantages for those aged 60 or over. Your local station will tell you more about the benefits.

Taking a bicycle on the train

Bicycles can be taken on some trains. But you will need to check in advance, and purchase the necessary ticket before boarding.

Bicycles can also be rented at many stations, either by the day or the week. Holders of rail tickets pay only a minimal fee. You'll need to supply proof of your identity, and pay a deposit which will be refunded when you return the bicycle to the station from which it was rented.

Learning some useful words and phrases

aankomst treinen uit de richting . . .	train arrivals from . . .
deuren openen	to open doors
duwen	push
naar overige sporen	to other platforms
niet instappen	do not board
noodrem	emergency brake
sluiten	to close
trekken	pull
verkoop binnenland	tickets to stations within the Netherlands
verkoop buitenland	tickets to stations outside the Netherlands
vertrek van de treinen	train departures

TRAVELLING BY TAXI

You cannot hail taxis in the street, but you will find ranks at many stations, and elsewhere in major cities. Alternatively, telephone a *taxicentrale* listed in your local telephone directory or *Yellow Pages* (*Gouden Gids*).

You may, however, find yourself in a queuing system, with a recorded message notifying you of the fact. If that happens, simply hold on until your call is answered.

An inexpensive option in many towns is the train taxi (*treintaxi*). These can be found at over 100 stations and cover over 400 provincial towns, cities and villages. A flat fee will take you anywhere within the town or city boundaries – although you may have to share if there are other passengers travelling in your direction.

You can buy a ticket at the station ticket office or from the conductor on the train, provided you have a valid train ticket.

It is also possible to book a train taxi to take you to the station, by ringing the *treintaxi-centrale* listed in the telephone directory. But you should allow plenty of time, and preferably book the day before. If you haven't bought a taxi ticket with your rail ticket in advance, you can buy one from the driver. But as the *treintaxi* is only for train travellers, he will charge you the flat fee plus an additional sum – and then give you a train gift voucher for that additional sum. You can then use this to help pay for your train ticket.

DRIVING IN THE NETHERLANDS

You must be aged 18 or over before you can drive a car in the Netherlands, but you may ride a moped from the age of 16. In general, drivers of all motor vehicles must be in possession of a driving licence. However, those born before 31.05.80 are permitted to use a moped without one.

Seat belts

Front seat belts must be worn by all adults, and by children over twelve. Rear seat belts must also be worn if available.

Children under twelve and less than 150 cm in height may only travel in a front seat if they have a seat specially adapted and approved for their size. (This applies even if the car has no rear seats.)

In rear seats, children up to three must be secured in a special child seat if there is one. Those aged between three and twelve must likewise be secured in a suitable child seat if there is one. If not, they must use any existing seat.

Drinking and driving

There are severe penalties for those with more than 0.05 per cent of alcohol in their blood. These include imprisonment as well as loss of licence.

Obtaining a Dutch driving licence

Holders of licences from EU countries

Holders of driving licences issued in other EU countries may use them to drive in the Netherlands for up to one year. Before that period has elapsed they must either apply for a Dutch licence or register their valid EU licence with the National Vehicle Administration Agency (*Rijksdienst voor het Wegverkeer*). In addition to their valid foreign driving licence, applicants will need two recent passport-size photographs, and proof that they have lived in the issuing country for at least 185 days.

If more than a year has elapsed, it is still possible to apply, but a medical certificate will also be required.

- Rijksdienst voor het Wegverkeer, Skager Rak 10, 9642 CZ Veendam, The Netherlands. Tel: (0598) 624240.

Holders of licences from non-EU countries

Holders of licences from non-EU countries must apply for a Dutch licence within six months. The Dutch embassy in your country of residence (or your country's embassy in the Netherlands) will be able to give you further information.

Learning the rules of the road

It is not possible to give a comprehensive summary of the Dutch rules of the road here. But the company VEKA Best publishes detailed information in various languages, including English (ISBN 9067990620). It can be ordered from bookshops if not in stock, or further information can be obtained from the publishers.

- VEKA Best, Donge 21, 5684 PX Best, The Netherlands.

In Britain, the AA also has some useful touring tips, available only to members. Simply ring their Information Centre on 0990 500 600 and quote your membership number.

- AA International Services, Automobile Association Developments Limited, Fanum House, Basing View, Basingstoke, Hampshire RG21 4EA, UK. Tel: (0990) 448866.

Some points to remember
Driving on the right
You must drive on the right and therefore you would normally overtake on the left. But where traffic is moving slowly in queues, overtaking on the right is permitted if it does not cause inconvenience to other traffic.

Filtering to the right is not permitted at controlled crossings unless the words *rechtsaf toegestaan* or a green arrow specifically indicate that you may do so.

Keeping to the speed limit
In general, the speed limit for cars, motorcycles and lorries in built-up areas is 50 kph (31 mph). Outside built-up areas, the limit for vehicles up to 3.5 tonnes is 120 kph (74 mph) on motorways, 100 kph (62 mph) on main roads (indicated by a white car on a blue background), and 80 kph (49 mph) on all other roads. The limit for lorries, coaches and vehicles with trailers is 80 kph on all roads outside built-up areas.

For mopeds, the speed limit in a built-up area is 30 kph (18 mph) and elsewhere 40 kph (24 mph).

Who has the right of way?
At an intersection, if the road ahead is a priority road (indicated by the triangular 'priority road ahead' sign, a STOP sign or a row of white triangles on the road itself), you must give way to any vehicle on that road – even a bicycle.

Otherwise, **you must give way to vehicles coming from the right**. Dutch drivers will assume that you are going to do this, and won't even slow down if they are the ones who have the right of way. So always take special care at unmarked intersections. The priority roads themselves are marked at frequent intervals by a yellow/orange diamond.

At roundabouts you should likewise give way to vehicles on the right (in other words, to vehicles **coming onto** the roundabout), unless otherwise indicated. The words *rotondeverkeer heeft voorrang* means that traffic on the roundabout has right of way.

Dealing with buses and trams
All other traffic has to **give way to buses** leaving bus stops in built-up areas. So when bus drivers signal that they are about to move out, you must allow them to do so.

There are special regulations regarding trams, too. Where roads of equal importance meet, for instance, trams have priority over all other traffic – even that coming from the right.

They are usually overtaken on the right. But if there is not enough space, you can overtake on the left, provided it is safe to do so. If the tram is stationary, watch out for people boarding or alighting. You may only pass on the right if you don't cause them any inconvenience.

Some hazards to watch out for
The sheer volume of cyclists can make driving in towns very unnerving. They may swerve suddenly or make other unexpected moves, and have a tendency to ignore road signs, including traffic lights. Be especially careful when opening car doors – even those on the right, as cyclists are permitted to overtake cars on the right, and will often slip between slow-moving traffic and the pavement.

If you are crossing the road on foot, you'll likewise need to beware of unseen cyclists slipping through tiny gaps.

A very different hazard is the dense autumn and winter fog, especially in the late evening and early morning.

CYCLING IN THE NETHERLANDS

Essential equipment
Bicycles in the Netherlands must be equipped with the following:

● a white light at the front

● a red light at the rear

● a red reflector at the rear

● orange reflectors on the pedals

● a white band at least 30 cm long on the rear mud guard

● a bell.

Helmets are not, however, compulsory.

On the road
Special regulations apply to cyclists.

● Unless you are on a priority road, you must give way to all motor traffic, whatever direction it is coming from.

● If there is a cycle track, you must use it. They are indicated by a white bicycle on a circular blue sign. (If a cycle lane is delineated by a solid white line, motor vehicles may not use it. But if there is a broken white line, motor vehicles can also drive there, as long as they do not obstruct the cyclists.)

- If a track is marked *fietspad* (cycle path), cyclists must use it, but mopeds are not permitted to do so unless the words *rijwielen met hulp-motor toegestaan* are also included on the sign.

- If there is no cycle track, you can cycle on the road, but not on motor-ways, or on roads reserved for motor vehicles (shown by a white car on a square blue sign).

- If you are on a cycle track, you may cross the road at places where two parallel rows of white squares have been painted on the surface.

- Children under eight can be carried on a special seat.

SOME USEFUL WORDS AND PHRASES

doorgaand verkeer	through traffic
doorgaand verkeer gestremd	no through road
lichten ontsteken	switch on your lights
matig uw snelheid	slow down
niet parkeren	no parking
omleiding	detour
uit	exit
uitrit vrijlaten	do not block exit
woonerven	speed ramps

CASE STUDIES

Susan gathers information
I went to the main bus and train stations soon after I arrived and asked them for information about the various tickets. I was amazed at how much you could save if you knew what you were doing. The bus services in major towns like this one are very good, too. They run frequently, and until late in the evening. So we rarely take the car into the centre of town. Parking is too much of a hassle.

Ian gets on his bike
It didn't take me long to discover that the quickest and cheapest way to get around Amsterdam is by bike. I bought one really cheaply from someone

who was going back to Scotland, and now I weave in and out of the traffic just like a native.

Kay and Jonathan take to the road

We shipped our car over from the US. But we were glad that other people in Jonathan's office could tell us how to deal with all the necessary regulations, We were also relieved that there was an English-language version of the rules of the road. Studying it made us feel much more confident.

CHECKLIST

1. How much do you think you would be able to use public transport in your working and social life?

2. Do you know which tickets will give you the best value?

3. How well do you think you will be able to adapt to driving conditions in the Netherlands?

5

Settling In

At first there is so much that seems strange. Even the smallest thing, like making a telephone call, can seem impossibly difficult. But once you've tried something once or twice, it soon becomes easier. And once you've mastered the everyday tasks, you'll feel much more at home.

GETTING PRACTICAL HELP

An organisation called ACCESS (Administrative Committee to Coordinate English-Speaking Services) could prove invaluable, especially if your Dutch is limited or non-existent. A non-profit organisation staffed entirely by a multi-national group of volunteers, they provide free information and help to the English-speaking community.

In addition to their bi-monthly newsletter, they sell a number of useful books and booklets (including their own excellent *Job Booklet*). But they also offer free information over the telephone on everything from the validity of driving licences to where to find an English-speaking doctor, dentist, lawyer or even babysitter.

Other activities (not free) include various workshops in English on such subjects as cross-cultural adjustment, having a baby in the Netherlands and careers. They also offer a counselling referral service to a wide range of English-speaking counsellors.

● ACCESS, Plein 24, 2511 CS Den Haag, The Netherlands. Tel: (070) 346 2525. Fax: (070) 356 1332.

DEALING WITH MONEY

The unit of currency in the Netherlands is the **guilder** (in English normally denoted by NLG, in Dutch by the symbol *f*).

The following coins are currently in circulation:

● *stuiver* = 5 cents

● *dubbeltje* = 10 cents

- *kwartje* = 25 cents

- *gulden* = 100 cents (or 1 guilder)

- *rijksdaalder* = 2.5 guilders

- *vijf gulden* = 5 guilders.

There are notes to the value of 10, 25, 50, 100, 250 and 1,000 guilders.

Paying without cash

Cheques are now rarely used for payments in shops, restaurants, filling stations, *etc*. Instead, *pinnen* – the use of a debit card in combination with a PIN number – has become widespread. You will be asked to key in your PIN number on the machine *(betaalautomaat)* provided. The amount is then debited from your account.

Sometimes your card will be swiped through the machine for you. Sometimes you must do it yourself, and then follow the instructions the machine gives you. A typical sequence would be:

1.	*Uw pas AUB*	Please swipe your card
2.	*Uw pincode AUB*	Please enter your pincode
3.	*Wacht op bedrag*	Wait for amount
4.	*Bedrag*	Amount
5.	*Akkoord toets Ja*	If you agree, press *Ja*
6.	*U heeft betaald*	You have paid.

For smaller amounts, up to 35 guilders, increasing use is being made of the *Chipper* or *Chipknip*. This is a sort of electronic purse, incorporated into a bankcard or *Europas*. You load this up at the special terminals which can be found next to cash dispensers (the amount is deducted from your account).

The amount you have loaded is shown electronically on your card, and you therefore don't have to key in your PIN number when paying in this way. After you have made your payment the terminal in the shop will tell you how much is left on your *Chipper*, so you know when to reload it.

Wilt u bij u Girorekening een Giropas ontvangen?	Do you want a Girocard with your Giro account?
Gaat u per maand ƒ1.000, - of meer aan inkomsten ontvangen op uw Girorekening?	Are you going to receive an income of 1,000 guilders a month or more in your Giro account?
Over uzelf	About you
Achternaam, voervoegsel	Surname, title
Man/vrouw	Male/female
Voornamen (voluit)	Forenames (in full)
Straat en nummer	Street and number
Postcode en plaats	Postcode and town
Telefoon privé/werk	Home/work telephone
Geboortedatum	Date of birth
Nationaliteit	Nationality
Andere, namelijk	Other, namely
Bent u 18 jaar of ouder?	Are you 18 years or older?
Heeft u al een Girorekening bij de Postbank?	Do you already have a Postbank Giro account?
Is de Girorekening alleen voor uzelf, of is de Girorekening voor twee personen?	Is the Giro account only for you, or is it for two people?
Over uw mede-aanvrager	About your fellow applicant
Handtekening van uzelf	Your signature
Datum van aanvraag	Date of application
In te vullen door medewerker postkantoor	To be completed by the post office

Fig. 4. Applying for a giro account – what the form means.

Opening a bank account

Major banks like the ABN-AMRO, the Rabobank and ING can be found all over the Netherlands, in town centres and in or near shopping centres.

The procedure for opening an account is generally the same whether you come from an EU or non-EU country. For private accounts, the process is a relatively easy and straight-forward one. You simply visit the branch you have choosen, taking with you some form of identification (such as your passport).

You may also be asked for evidence that you have a residence permit, and that it is valid for longer than six months. Or you may have to provide a statement from your employer that you will be working in the Netherlands for a certain period.

The bank will then make the necessary enquiries via computer, and if there are no negative indications the account will be opened.

Business accounts need additional documents. But any bank will gladly give a list of requirements.

It's worth asking if your bank has any literature in English, too. If they don't have any at the branch, they may be able to obtain some for you.

Using a bank account

You will receive transfer forms (*overschrijvingsformulieren*) to enable you to transfer money to other accounts (see the Paying Bills section below).

You can also apply for various types of card, including a *Europas* with PIN number and *Chipknip* or *Chipper* (see page 46). This will enable you to withdraw money from cash machines and to make payments in many shops, garages and restaurants. In addition, you can use it to withdraw money in an increasing number of other countries, and it can be used in combination with Eurocheques, which are valid in many European countries.

If you lose a *Europas,* you should inform the police, and also call 0800-0313 to report the loss as soon as possible. Fraudulent use of your card will then be almost impossible.

Opening a Postbank giro account

The Postbank offers many of the services offered by banks, with the advantage that there are no charges for most services as long as you stay in credit. Many Dutch nationals never have an account with a bank, finding that the Postbank (a service provided by the Dutch Post Office) serves all their needs.

Postbank customers can now also withdraw cash both at post offices and from bank cash machines, making the service even more attractive.

To open a Postbank giro account *(girorekening),* you will need to fill in the form obtainable from any post office. Then take it to any post office along with your passport. The translations given in Figure 4 should help

Filling in an *overschrivingsformulier*

Naar bankrekening of girorekening	To account number
Ten name van	In the name of
Plaats	Town
Bedrag	Amount
Betalingskenmerk/Faktuurnummer	Reference/Invoice number
Mededelingen	Messages
Handtekening	Signature
De ruimte hieronder niet beschrijven en het formulier niet vouwen	Do not write in the space below and do not fold

Understanding an Acceptgiro

Deze strook niet meezenden	Do not send this counterfoil
Over te schrijven/te storten	(Amount) to be transferred/deposited
Van girorekening . . . of van bankrekening	From giro account . . . or from bank account
van/door	Of/by
naam	Name
adres	(Street) address
plaats	Town
op rekening	To account (number)
tgv	For the benefit of
formulier met blauwe of zwarte inkt invullen	Use blue or black ink to fill in form
zijn alle rode rubrieken ingevuld?	Are all red sections completed?
Handtekening	Signature
de ruimte hieronder niet beschrijven	Do not write in the space below

Fig. 5. Making payments.

with the completion of this form. But any post office clerk will also help you with any problems you may have.

Using your giro account

At the post office you will be given further information about your Giro account. *Overschrijvingskaarten* (transfer cards), which you can use to transfer money from your account to someone else's, will then be sent to your home (see the Paying Bills section below). You will also receive the Girofoon code, which enables you to transfer money to other Giro and bank accounts by telephone, and also to obtain information about your balance. If you have asked for a Giro card (*Giropas*), you will also be notified when you can collect it. The card enables you to make payments and also withdraw money in both the Netherlands and abroad. Like the *Europas*, it comes with a *Chipper* (see page 46).

You can obtain further information by calling 0800-0400 (free).

If you lose your guarantee card, you should call (058) 212 6000 immediately.

Using an automatic cash dispenser

If you insert a foreign card into a cash machine, you will be asked which language you want the instructions to be in, and they are easily followed. If you are using a Dutch account, the usual procedure is as follows:

1. Insert your card into the machine as shown.

2. Key in your PIN number.

3. Look at the screen and, if requested, press the relevant button(s) to indicate what you require: *Geldopname* = withdrawal, *Saldoinformatie* = account balance. (This step is not always included.)

4. In the case of a withdrawal, you will next be asked to indicate how much you wish to withdraw, and then whether you want a *transsactiebon* (withdrawal advice).

5. Remove your card.

6. Remove your money.

7. Wait for your withdrawal advice if you asked for one.

If you are asked the question *Akkoord?*, it means 'Do you agree?'. If you do, press the *Akkoord* button.

Paying bills

Many bills are paid by means of a credit transfer directly into the account of the company issuing the bill. If you have a Postbank account, this will be by means of an *overschrijvingskaart,* which you complete and send to the Postbank in one of the envelopes provided. If you have a bank account, you will use an *overschrijvingsformulier,* which you simply complete and send to your bank.

Typical information that you will be asked to fill in is again given in Figure 5.

Automatic payment of regular bills can also be arranged.

Dealing with an *Acceptgiro*

Many companies will send you a so-called *Acceptgiro* form in order to make payment easier. Their account details, and often the amount to be paid, will be printed on it.

If your own account details are also known to them (as they will be in the case of regular bills like electricity, gas and telephone) then these, too, will be pre-printed. So all you have to do is sign the form and send it to your bank or Postbank. Otherwise, you will need to fill these in.

Obtaining credit cards

Banks, including the Postbank, also have credit cards. Costs and conditions vary. Your bank or post office will give you further details.

USING THE TELEPHONE

You can dial most countries direct, so using a private telephone presents no problems. You will hear a dialling tone when you lift the receiver. For calls within the Netherlands, simply dial the area code, immediately followed by the remainder of the number. But if the number your are dialling has the same area code as your own, you omit that part of the number.

For international calls, dial 00 + the country code, and then dial the remainder of the number.

You'll find all the country codes in any telephone directory. That for the UK is 44. For the US and Canada, the country code is 1. Australia's code is 61 and that for New Zealand is 64. But for the UK, Australia and New Zealand (and many other countries), you must also remember to delete the initial 0 from the inland number.

Installing a telephone

Private customers can apply for a new telephone line at the Primafoon telephone shops found all over the country, or at post offices or official KPN

Telecom dealers. Take along your passport as identification.

Applications for business telephones can be made at Business Centres, or again at post offices and official KPN Telecom dealers.

If you do not speak Dutch, ask an assistant to help you fill in the form and to explain the various tariffs available.

Bills will be sent every two months, in the form of an *Acceptgiro*. You should pay promptly. Only one reminder will be sent before the phone is disconnected.

Obtaining telephone directories

You'll receive a local phone directory *(telefoongids)* some time during the first three months of the year. If yours is not delivered, telephone 0800-0402 (free) to ask for one.

You can also order extra directories. Ask for the folder *Extra Telefoongidsen* at a Primafoon telephone shop, or telephone 0800 0402.

Every subscriber also receives a copy of the local *Yellow Pages (Gouden Gids)* each year. It is also possible to purchase *Yellow Pages* for other areas. Telephone (020) 567 6500 for details.

Using a Dutch telephone directory

Subscribers' names are listed alphabetically, but where there is more than one subscriber with the same surname, they are listed in alphabetical order of street name. So K Haarsma of Amsterdamstraat will be listed before A Haarsma of Stationsweg.

Prefixes are treated like initials. So a name like S de Vries would be listed under V, not D, and K van de Graaf would be under G.

Since the letters ij are another form of the letter y, you'll find names containing them listed with those containing a y. So, for example, you'll find the name IJsselstein under the Ys, and a name like Keijzer with all the Keyzers.

Phoning directory enquiries

If you don't know a number, and you do not have the relevant telephone directory, you can obtain the number from directory enquiries. For numbers within the Netherlands, dial 118. Give the name, street address and town of the person whose number you are seeking and the computer will give you the number.

Alternatively, if you do not have the complete address, you can speak to an operator by dialling 0800 8008. This costs more, but you can ask for up to six numbers. You can also use this number to ask for addresses and post-codes of companies. For international numbers, dial 0800-0418. You may ask for at most two numbers at once.

Sometimes your call will be placed in a queuing system and you will hear a recorded announcement telling you how many people are waiting in front

Dutch	International
Anna	Amsterdam
Bernard	Baltimore
Cornelis	Casablanca
Dirk	Denmark
Eduard	Edison
Ferdinand	Florida
Gerard	Gallipoli
Hendrik	Havana
Izaak	Italy
Jan	Jerusalem
Karel	Kilogramme
Leonard	Liverpool
Marie	Madagascar
Nico	New York
Otto	Oslo
Pieter	Paris
Quotiënt	Quebec
Rudolf	Rome
Simon	Santiago
Theodor	Tripoli
Utrecht	Uppsala
Victor	Valencia
Willem	Washington
Xantippe	Xantippe
Ypsilon	Yokohama
Zaandam	Zurich

Fig. 6. The telephone alphabet.

of you. (For instance, *Er zijn nog drie wachtenden voor U,* or 'There are three people in front of you.')

If you have to spell a name, it helps to know the telephone alphabet. You'll find two versions of this (a Dutch and an international one) in Figure 6.

Using '06' numbers

There are several kinds of telephone numbers beginning with 06. Those beginning with 06-0 and 06-4 are free. There are charges (sometimes high ones) for the others.

To avoid confusion changes have been taking place, however, and eventually 06 numbers will be used only for mobile phones. Most free numbers now have 0800 codes, while 0900, 0906 and 0909 codes indicate premium rates.

Calling from a public telephone

In most cases, you should find that clear instructions for using the telephone are given in English.

Using a card phone

Many boxes use telephone cards, and you will have to buy one in advance from a post office or from one of the special machines. The location of the nearest supplier will be included with the operating instructions printed above the phone.

The usual procedure for using one of these phones is to:

● lift the receiver

● place the card in the slot

● dial

● speak

● replace the receiver

● remove the card.

If, however, the phone also accepts credit cards, you will place your credit card in a different slot, and remove it before dialling.

Using a coin-operated phone

Boxes which still use coins will accept *kwartjes* (25 cents), guilders, *rijksdaalders* (2.5 guilders) and five-guilder coins. Unused money is returned when the call is finished. So you can insert as much as you like to ensure that your call is not interrupted by the money running out. Always include some small denomination coins, though. If the money remaining at the end of your call is *f*4.25, and the only coins you have used are five-guilder ones, you will not receive your change.

To make a call, lift the receiver, insert coins, dial and speak. If you wish to make a second call, press the receiver hook briefly and then dial the new number. When you have finished, replace the receiver and any unused coins will be returned.

The phone will disconnect instantly when the money runs out. So during a longer call, you may need to keep adding money to ensure that this doesn't happen. The amount remaining is shown on a screen, so you will know when it is getting low.

Some useful numbers

Emergency (police/fire/ambulance)	112
Directory enquiries (inland)	118 or 0800-8008
Directory enquiries (international)	0800-0418
To report a fault	0800-0407
Account queries	0800-0404
Weather (inland)	0900-8003
Time	0900-8002
Traffic information (inland)	0900-9622
Public transport information	0900-9292

LEARNING THE LANGUAGE

Most Dutch people speak some English. Many speak it really well, and some English-speaking residents never bother to learn Dutch at all. But the more Dutch you are able to speak, the more at home you will feel – and you will certainly increase your work prospects.

For some jobs, like nursing, a certain degree of proficiency is an absolute prerequisite. But even if all your colleagues have English as their mother tongue, you will still find that learning the language has its advantages. You can feel very isolated and frustrated if you have no idea what is going on around you. And you'll find that Dutch people are invariably delighted that you've taken the trouble to learn – even if it's just a few words.

Taking classes before you go

Ask the Dutch embassy in your own country whether they have a list of colleges offering classes in the Dutch language. The Royal Netherlands Embassy in London, for instance, should be able to send you a list of day and evening classes in London for both beginners and more advanced students.

- Royal Netherlands Embassy, Cultural Affairs Department, 38 Hyde Park Gate, London SW7 5DP, UK. Tel: (020) 7590 3200.

Berlitz has centres all over the world, most of which offer Dutch tuition. There are six centres in Britain – in London, Birmingham, Manchester, Edinburgh, Brighton and Baldock (Herts) – as well as more than 60 in the US and eight in Canada.

- The Berlitz School of Languages Limited, 9-13 Grosvenor Street, London W1A 3BZ, UK. Tel: (020) 7915 0909. Fax: (020) 7915 0222.

Many other language schools throughout the world will likewise include Dutch courses in their programmes.

Using book and cassette courses

An alternative would be to **teach yourself** some basic Dutch with the help of books and/or cassettes.

Linguaphone, for instance, have two Dutch courses for English speakers – a starter course, covering basic essentials, and a more comprehensive Language Course Plus. Each includes both cassettes and accompanying course books.

- Linguaphone, Carlton Place, 111 Upper Richmond Road, London SW15 2TJ, UK. Tel: (020) 8333 4852. Fax: (020) 8333 4897.

Hugo's Language Books also have a number of books and audio courses for Dutch learners. These include a basic *On the Move* cassette-only course. The *Dutch in Three Months* book is available on its own or with a cassette course. And the *Complete Audio Course* combines *Dutch in Three Months* with the more advanced *Taking Dutch Further*. All are available through bookshops.

- Hugo's Language Books Ltd, Redvers House, 13 Fairmile, Henley-on-Thames, Oxfordshire RG9 2JR, UK. Tel: (01491) 572656. Fax: (01491) 573590.

Finding classes in the Netherlands

You will find many **language schools** in the Netherlands offering Dutch courses to English speakers. The Dutch embassy in your own country or your own country's embassy in the Netherlands should be able to send you a list of some of them. Or you can contact the information service ACCESS mentioned at the beginning of this chapter.

If there is more than one school within easy reach of where you are living, contact several to compare not only prices but also the range of courses they offer (language laboratory, private tuition, or a combination of the two, for instance). Some offer intensive 'survival' courses, or special courses for those in business.

The Foreign Student Service also publishes a country-wide guide to *Non-university Dutch language courses in the Netherlands* at a modest charge.

● Foreign Student Service, Oranje Nassaulaan 5, 1075 AH Amsterdam, The Netherlands. Tel: (020) 671 5915.

In addition, Amsterdam's Volksuniversiteit offers a very wide range of courses, ranging from those for beginners to very advanced classes. Unlike those at the language laboratories, these run for a fixed period of 12 weeks, with classes once, twice or three times a week. As they are very intensive, only those with at least ten years of schooling in their own country are admitted.

● Volksuniversiteit Amsterdam, Rapenburgerstraat 73, 1011 VK Amsterdam, The Netherlands. Tel: (020) 626 1626.

CASE STUDIES

Susan makes herself at home
I learnt some Dutch before I came here, which was essential for my job as a nurse. I started off with a simple book and cassette course. But once I'd decided I was going to come and live here, I invested in a course at a language school. It made life so much easier after I arrived. Not only did the course teach me a lot of Dutch words and phrases. It also contained a lot of information about everyday life here.

Ian continues to rely on his friends
As most of my friends are English-speaking, and I don't know how long I'll be staying, I haven't bothered to learn much Dutch. Although I've picked up a few words through my job at the snack bar.

It does make things a bit difficult sometimes. But there's usually someone around who can help me out if I get stuck. And I'm amazed at how much information is available in English here.

I didn't have a bank account or anything at first, as there didn't seem to be much point. But then I ended up having to open one in a hurry when I found my first job. Now I wish I'd gone for a giro account, but it doesn't seem worth changing.

Kay learns quickly

When we first arrived it all seemed so strange. Not just the language, but every little thing was different. At first, even finding a phone number took forever.

But there are a lot of other expats working for the same company as Jonathan, so there was always someone to ask. And Jonathan had been sent on an intensive Dutch course before we left, so that helped. I enrolled with a language school soon after we arrived and now, although many of our friends are also English speakers, I feel much more at home.

Diane does things the Dutch way

As my husband was Dutch, he insisted that I open a giro account instead of a bank account. And I was glad I did. It's handy being able to withdraw money from the post office, as there's one very close to where I live. And I can use bank machines to obtain money as well. Added to which, all the services I use regularly are free, however many transactions I make. When you are on a low income, every little helps.

CHECKLIST

1. Do you need a bank account, or would a Postbank *girorekening* suit your needs better?

2. Do you know what an *Acceptgiro* is, and what to do when you get one?

3. Do you think you will need to learn Dutch and, if so, which method would suit you best?

6

Setting Up Home

There is a chronic shortage of housing in the Netherlands, especially of less expensive accommodation. So you may have to arrange temporary lodgings while you look for something more permanent.

The local tourist office (or *VVV*) will be able to give you information about hotels in all price ranges, as well as local bed and breakfast addresses, youth hostels and so on. You'll find the address and telephone number of your nearest *VVV* in the telephone directory.

DECIDING WHETHER TO RENT OR BUY

Whether you decide to rent or buy will depend to a large extent on how long you plan to stay in the Netherlands, as well as on your financial circumstances and employment situation.

One advantage of buying is that your mortgage interest will be deducted from your taxable income. But the costs involved in buying a house are high. Tax has to be paid every time a house changes hands, and there are legal fees as well as those payable to the estate agent. So unless you are staying in the country for several years, you will not recoup your outlay.

Even if you plan a long stay, you may decide to rent for a while to give you the chance to look around properly before buying.

RENTING A ROOM

If you are on your own, you may decide simply to rent a room for a while. But you will not find it easy to find somewhere suitable. Many people find rooms through friends, so tell everyone you know that you are looking for somewhere.

Sometimes rooms are advertised in shop windows or on noticeboards. Look for a sign saying *Te Huur Aangeboden* (see Figure 7).

Advertisements also appear in local newspapers. But you will have to be quick off the mark in order to find somewhere.

Te Huur Aangeboden

RUIME FLAT met lift, cv en zonnig balkon. Ind: woonkamer, sl.kmr, keuken, douche/toilet, hal. Hr. ƒ1.000, - p.m. Tel. (000) 000 0000 na 18.00 uur.

Onroerend goed

AMSTERDAMSEWEG 111: Benedenwoning met c.v. Ind: woonkamer, 2 sl.kmrs, keuken, douche, toilet, bergruimte. ƒ275.000, - k.k. Inl: (000) 000 0000.

To let

SPACIOUS FLAT with lift, central heating and sunny balcony. Comprising: living room, bedroom, shower/toilet, kitchen, hall. Rent: ƒ1000 per month. Tel: (000) 000 0000 after 6.00 p.m.

Real estate

AMSTERDAMSEWEG 111: Ground-floor home with central heating. Comprising: living room, two bedrooms, kitchen, shower, toilet, storage space. ƒ275,000. Information: (000) 000 0000.

Fig. 7. Classified advertisements for a flat to rent and a home for sale.

RENTING A FLAT OR HOUSE

Again, friends can be a useful source of information about places for rent. You will also find advertisements in newspapers, and in shop windows or on noticeboards. But even if you find a place to rent in this way, you may not be allowed to live in it.

Applying for a housing permit

The severe shortage of housing in the Netherlands means that you will need to obtain a housing permit (*woonvergunning*) in order to rent many houses or flats. Rents are strictly controlled, and if the rent is below a certain level only those with permits are eligible. Your local municipality (*gemeente*) can tell you the situation in your own locality.

In many places, you must be registered with the *gemeente* for several years before you can hope to receive a permit. And there are usually other conditions, such as a requirement that you are 'economically bound' to an area – in other words, that your work forces you to live there. If you are self-employed, or work in another town, you will not fulfil this condition.

Using an estate agent

Many foreigners find it easier to use the services of an estate agent (*makelaar*). These tend to deal only in more expensive accommodation, for which no *woonvergunning* is required. But many foreigners – especially new arrivals – are not eligible for the less expensive houses and flats in any case.

The *Nederlandse Vereniging van Makelaars in onroerende goederen* (the Netherlands Estate Agents Federation, or *NVM*) will send you details of their members in your part of the country. And they also have a useful booklet, in English, entitled *You and your NVM-broker*. It explains the role of the estate agent and outlines their code of conduct. When using a broker, however, make sure you discuss the procedure and fees before you start, so that you know exactly what is involved.

● Nederlandse Vereniging van Makelaars o.g. en vastgoeddeskundigen NVM, Postbus 2222, 3430 DC Nieuwegein, The Netherlands. Tel: (030) 608 5185. Fax: (030) 608 5185.

You will probably have to pay a deposit of at least one month's rent. This will be refunded when you leave, provided that you leave everything in good condition.

Rents are usually due on the first day of the month. So you should make arrangements for your bank to transfer the payments at least seven to eight days before that.

What will be provided?

Furnished (*gemeubileerd*) accommodation is not common in the Netherlands. If, however, you do rent furnished accommodation, you would expect it to contain absolutely everything, including china, cutlery, saucepans and even linen.

In general, unfurnished accommodation (*ongemeubileerd*) really is an empty shell. You have to provide everything from carpets and curtains to beds, chairs, tables, cupboards and electrical appliances like cooker and fridge. Even electrical fittings like light sockets usually have to be provided by you, as well as all the light bulbs.

There is also occasionally something known as *gestoffeerd* accommodation. This will include floor coverings and curtains. But you should check whether anything else is included as well.

You will also need to enquire whether there are service charges, and whether these include hot water and central heating. If not, is there a water heater that you can rent or buy from the previous occupant? Or will you have to provide one?

You should check whether gas and electricity are included, too. Normally these charges are paid directly to the utility companies. But very occasionally they may be included in the rent, which will then naturally be higher to allow for this.

Carrying out repairs and maintenance

Internal decoration will probably be your responsibility, as will the repair of any damage that you cause. Your contract will clarify exactly what your **liabilities** are, and you should check it carefully, asking for explanations of any terms you don't understand. External decoration and repair of damage that is not your fault should be carried out by the landlord.

Avoiding some of the pitfalls

- Make sure that your contract includes a clause allowing you to leave with two months' notice. You don't want to find yourself liable to four more years' rent when your employer transfers you out of the country.

- Make sure that there is no clause giving the landlord the right to reoccupy the premises.

- If you use an estate agent or broker, make sure that all the negotiating of prices and terms is done through them, and not directly between you and the owner or landlord. Verbal agreements are binding.

- Prepare an inventory of everything left in the flat or house, and its condition, and have it signed by both parties. This can save you a great deal of acrimony when you leave, and are charged for the replacement of the three broken door handles which have irritated you since the day you arrived.

● Check all walls, windows, doors *etc.* and if you find any damage, make sure that this, too, is noted in your inventory.

● If central heating is provided, make sure that it is in working order.

BUYING A FLAT OR HOUSE

Renting is the choice of by far the majority of those intending to stay for only a limited period. But if you have a long-term contract, or are even planning to stay indefinitely, then you may choose to buy. The various additional costs involved usually amount to about 10-14 per cent of the purchase price. So you want to be sure that you will be staying long enough to recoup this.

In some areas you will need a housing permit (*woonvergunning*) before you can buy a property below a certain (fairly high) price, and you may need to be 'economically bound' to the area. Your local municipality will be able to tell you more about the whole, very complicated, system.

Most purchasers make use of an estate agent (*makelaar*), who will not only help you find a property but also guide you through all the stages involved in buying. Again, the NVM mentioned above will send you a list of members.

What your *makelaar* will do

If you employ a qualified *makelaar* to help you through the house-buying maze, the services he offers are comprehensive. He will:

● seek out all properties fitting your requirements

● view any of interest with you

● advise you on the condition of the house that you choose (it is not usual to use an independent surveyor)

● negotiate the price for you

● draft the purchase deed in most cases, and handle other paperwork

● advise on financing.

In return, he will charge a commission for his services, which you should agree in advance.

Obtaining a mortgage

Various types of mortgage (*hypotheek*) are available, with new ones appearing all the time. Your *makelaar* may offer independent advice on finding the one that best suits your needs, but you should check in advance whether there is any charge for this. It may also pay to shop around.

Advice can also be obtained from specialist mortgage advisors (*hypotheekadviseurs*). Banks have brochures on the various mortgages they can offer.

Interest rates vary. The usual repayment period is 25 or 30 years, but shorter periods can also be agreed.

The purchasing process

Your *makelaar* will guide you through the whole process. He will tell you what he thinks the price of your chosen property should be. You then make an offer – generally less than the full amount you are prepared to pay. After some negotiation, a verbal agreement will be reached, and you should remember that in the Netherlands this is legally binding.

A written contract will then be drawn up and signed, and you will be expected to pay a deposit at the office of a notary public (*notaris*). The remainder will be payable on completion.

The notary public will check that there are no claims on the house, and your *makelaar* will check all the papers. Then both buyer and seller must attend a meeting with a notary public to complete the transfer of the property. (Your *makelaar* should attend this meeting with you.)

The *notaris* will charge a fixed fee for his work, and will also pass on to the purchaser his search fees and the fee for registering the transfer in the public register (*kadaster*). In addition, a transfer tax amounting to six per cent of the purchase price is payable by the purchaser (although some contracts now specify that this charge should be divided between purchaser and vendor).

RUNNING YOUR NEW HOME

Gas, electricity and water

Both gas and electricity are supplied by the *Gemeente Energiebedrijf* (Municipal Energy Company, *GEB*), whose address and phone number are in the telephone directory.

Bills are sent out every two months, based on an annual meter reading. If, at the end of the year, you are found to have underpaid, you will be sent a bill for the balance. If you have paid too much, the overpayment will be deducted from your next bill. If the amount overpaid is more than the amount due on your next bill, the balance is repaid to you.

The electricity supply is 220 volts, 50 Hz, three-phase. You should **check before shipping** whether your appliances can be used. Most US appliances will need a transformer, for instance. And some, like stereos, cannot be used at all.

You will also have to pay for water and an environmental tax (*milieu-heffing*), and there is an annual *rioolbelasting* for connection to the sewer system.

Disposing of refuse

Ask your neighbours to tell you about collection days, or contact the Municipal Maintenance Department (listed in the telephone directory under (*Gemeente instellingen – dienst stadsbeheer*). You may have to use separate containers for biodegradable and non-biodegradable materials, and they may be collected on different days.

The Dutch set great store by recycling. So you may also be expected to make use of nearby recycling containers for paper and glass. There could be up to three containers for glass, so you should ensure that you use the correct one for clear glass (white container), for green or for brown. A yellow container can be used for all colours of glass.

If you need to dispose of particularly large items (*grof vuil*), the same municipal department will be able to tell you the procedure and any associated fees. There will also be special arrangements for the collection of chemical waste, like batteries and dirty oil.

Paying property tax

You have to pay property tax (*onroerendgoed belasting*) on any property owned or used by you. If you are a property owner, this means you pay twice – once as an owner and again because you are the user of the property.

Insuring your home

You need to arrange insurance cover for any home that you buy, and it is advisable to cover contents as well. Your *makelaar*, bank or an insurance adviser (*verzekeringsadviseur*) will be able to advise you.

Acquiring a TV and radio licence

If you have a television and/or radio you no longer need to buy a licence.

overseas. Again, jobs in the Netherlands can be few and far between. But from time to time, shortages can occur and then the number will increase.

If you live in a major city, look out, too, for Saturday editions of major Dutch newspapers, which often carry large numbers of job advertisements.

Making use of existing contacts

If your present employer has an office in the Netherlands, you can always enquire about the possibilities of a transfer within the company. Or maybe your work regularly brings you into contact with firms in the Netherlands. Could there be any openings there?

Are you a member of a **professional organisation**? If so, can they tell you anything about the employment prospects in the Netherlands? Can they put you in contact with the equivalent Dutch organisation, or do they have a list of Dutch companies that you could contact?

Contacting the relevant professional organisation in the Netherlands can be particularly useful. When a shortage of skilled employees occurs in a particular profession in the Netherlands, advertisements may eventually appear in the specialist press in the UK. But the relevant professional organisation in the Netherlands may foresee the demand long before that.

Casting the net wide

Tell everyone you know or meet that you are looking for work in the Netherlands. You never know who may have a Dutch sister-in-law, or a friend who works for a major international company in Amsterdam.

You could also contact recruitment agencies in your field, or seek out management consultants who have links with the Netherlands.

Bilateral Chambers of Commerce may be able to provide certain lists of companies in the Netherlands – but these can be costly, especially to non-members. At the time of writing, for instance, the Netherlands British Chamber of Commerce offers details of 490 British-owned companies based in the Netherlands. But the price to non-members is £80.

● Netherlands British Chamber of Commerce, The Dutch House, 307-308 High Holborn, London WC1V 7LS, UK. Tel: (020) 7405 1358. Fax: (020) 7405 1689.

Writing to possible employers 'on spec' from another country can, in any case, be extremely disheartening. You can expect that only a very small percentage will even reply.

EVALUATING QUALIFICATIONS

If you have any academic or professional qualifications, it could be vital to your job-seeking success to have diplomas evaluated to see whether they will be recognised in the Netherlands. I was once turned down for a job requiring only basic numeracy, because my education was insufficient. I had a first class mathematics degree. But the company's personnel department had recorded only my primary school education, since they did not recognise any of my examination certificates.

Academic and vocational qualifications

The process of having a diploma verified is known in Dutch as *diplomavergelijking* or *diplomawaardering*. Several Dutch agencies carry this out, but your first port of call should be your local *Adviseur voor Opleiding en Beroep (AOB)*. These can be found in most cities. Simply telephone them (this is better than calling in) and they will send you a list of instructions and an application form or *aanmeldingsformulier*.

They may then refer you to another organisation, such as NUFFIC, which evaluates higher academic qualifications. Other cases might be referred to COLO (*Centraal Orgaan van de Landelijke Opleidsorganen*), which is the Centre of Expertise for the international comparison of vocational qualifications. But COLO does not carry out evaluations for private individuals directly, so you must first contact your local *AOB* office.

- NUFFIC, Postbus 29777, 2502 LT Den Haag, The Netherlands. Tel: (070) 426 0260. Fax: (070) 426 0399.

- Centraal Orgaan van de Landelijke Opleidingsorganen (COLO), Postbus 7259, 2701 AG Zoetermeer, The Netherlands. Tel: (079) 352 3000. Fax: (079) 351 5478.

In the UK, NARIC (National Academic Recognition Information Centre) provides information on broad equivalence of qualifications for academic purposes.

- NARIC, Ecctis 2000 Ltd, Oriel House, Oriel Road, Cheltenham, Gloucestershire GL50 1XP, UK. Tel: (01242) 260010.

Professional qualifications

If you are a resident of an EU country, yours could be one of the many recognised professions, which would mean that you could practise in the Netherlands without re-qualifying. **Doctors, nurses, architects** and **vets** are among those whose qualifications are recognised – although in many cases you **will** need to learn Dutch if you are to have any chance of finding work.

Your professional organisation should be able to give you more infor-

Scanning the small ads

Saturday editions of major Dutch newspapers like *De Volkskrant, Algemeen Dagblad* and *De Telegraaf* generally carry a large number of job advertisements, as do many regional newspapers. Look out especially for advertisements from international companies, and of course for advertisements in English which indicate that a good knowledge of the English language is required (see Figure 8).

The weekly *Intermediair* has numerous advertisements for professional positions. It is also worth keeping an eye on foreign newspapers. And look out for professional publications in your own field. Even if you cannot understand the articles, you should soon be able to make some sense out of any job advertisements.

Registering with private agencies

There are numerous private agencies offering temporary work in the Netherlands. You'll find them listed in the *Yellow Pages* (*Gouden Gids*) under the heading *Uitzendbureaux*. But the numbers can be overwhelming. Try ringing a few to see whether they would be likely to have anything for you. Some well-known names are, Content, Manpower, Randstad, Tempo-Team and Unique, but there are many more.

You could also ask the *Algemene Bond Uitzendondernemingen* to send you a list of member agencies, and then contact a few to see which have branches in the area where you wish to work.

● Algemene Bond Uitzendondernemingen (ABU), Postbus 302, 1170 AH Badhoevedorp, Amsterdam, The Netherlands. Tel: (020) 658 0101.

In general, you will find few openings for someone who doesn't speak any Dutch. But a few agencies do specialise in placing English-speakers. If you have secretarial or clerical experience, for instance, you could contact Job-In in The Hague, or Undutchables in Amsterdam, Rotterdam and Utrecht, and you'll find a number of others mentioned in *The Job Booklet*.

● Job-In Uitzendbureau, Javastraat 35a, 2585 AD Den Haag, The Netherlands. Tel: (070) 363 5120. Fax: (070) 363 3851.

● Undutchables, Postbus 57204, 1040 BC Amsterdam, The Netherlands. Tel: (020) 623 1300.

● Undutchables, Oudehoofdplein 4, 3011 TM Rotterdam, The Netherlands. Tel: (010) 404 6650.

● Undutchables, Oudegracht 44, 3511 AR Utrecht, The Netherlands. Tel: (030) 238 2228.

What you will need before registering

- an up-to-date CV (you may be asked to have it translated into Dutch)

- passport

- residence permit

- *SOFI* number (see Chapter 3)

- the name and address of your health insurance fund (*Ziekenfonds*) and the policy number

- passport photos in case you are asked for one

- bank or giro account number

- any relevant certificates and diplomas.

Take photocopies of all the necessary documents, so that you can leave one with each agency you approach.

Seasonal work
You could contact your local employment office to see if there is any seasonal work in your own area. Bulb picking is one possibility between June and September. The *KAVB (Koninklijke Algemeene Vereeniging voor Bloembollencultuur)* can supply the names of firms that may be looking for seasonal help.

- Koninklijke Algemeene Vereeniging voor Bloembollencultuur (KAVB), Postbus 175, 2180 AD Hillegom, The Netherlands. Tel: (0252) 515 254. Fax: (0252) 519 714.

Some other possibilities for English-speakers
Try contacting your country's embassy or consulate to see if there are any vacancies (although many have few openings for those from outside the Netherlands).

Teachers may be able to find work (full-time, part-time or supply teaching) with one of the various English-speaking schools established in the Netherlands – or with one of the Dutch schools that have an English stream. You'll find some addresses in Chapter 9 and in the Useful Addresses section. But a complete list can be found on the website of the Foundation for International Education (*Stichting Internationaal Onderwijs*) at www.sio.nl.

Alternatively, if you have a **TEFL** (Teaching English as a Foreign Language) certificate, you could try some of the language schools (see Chapter 5).

If you are a **nurse**, contact hospitals in your area (armed with all the necessary documents to confirm the validity of your qualifications in the Netherlands – and, of course, with a good knowledge of Dutch).

If you have experience with a particular kind of company in another country, try writing to similar companies in the Netherlands. (Again, it helps if you know some Dutch.) And try joining some of the organisations for expatriates (see Chapter 11). Those who have successfully fought their own way through the job-seeking jungle are usually happy to let new arrivals benefit from their own experience.

Working as an au pair

A number of agencies in the UK and elsewhere send au pairs to the Netherlands and some organise additional activities for au pairs, too. Au pairs working for Activity International in the Netherlands, for instance, automatically become members of their Go Dutch Club, which organises days out, first aid courses and weekend trips. They also provide their au pairs with an informative *Survival Manual*, which includes hints on handling Dutch children as well as general information about life in the Netherlands.

● Activity International, Steentilstraat 25, 9711 GK Groningen, The Netherlands. Tel: (050) 313 0666.

Voluntary work

If you are unable to find work, and are not dependent on an income from employment, voluntary work might help to fill the gap – possibly enabling you to learn new skills and improve your Dutch as well as providing fulfilment. And you could even find that it leads directly to paid employment in the long run.

Contact the Netherlands Centre for Voluntary Work (*De Nederlandse Organisatie Vrijwilligerswerk*) for further information, including the address of your nearest *Vrijwilligers Centrale* (Volunteers Centre) and *Vrijwilligers Vacature Bank*, which lists both organisations seeking volunteers and people seeking voluntary work.

● De Nederlandse Organisatie Vrijwilligerswerk, Information and Documentation Department, Postbus 2877, 3500 GW Utrecht, The Netherlands. Tel: (030) 231 9844.

ACCESS also has information on volunteer work, some of which is contained in *The Job Booklet*.

SETTING UP YOUR OWN BUSINESS

Another option you could consider (especially if you are unable to find suitable work within a company) is whether you could set up some kind of business of your own. This could be just a one-person concern – perhaps offering some kind of service on a freelance basis. Or maybe you have an idea for a venture that would offer employment to a number of others as well. In either case, you'll find that there are plenty of sources of help and advice.

In addition, if you are self-employed with no employees, or if you work freelance, you should not need a work permit – even if you are from a non-EU country. But you will need to contact your local Chamber of Commerce (*Kamer van Koophandel*) to make sure that you satisfy any legal requirements.

So take a look at your skills and interests and see whether any of them could provide you with an income:

● Could you make something that others might want to buy?

● Could you import something from your own country that would be of interest to Dutch people or other expatriates?

● Is there something you could teach, like aerobics or English or some kind of craft?

● Could you offer your services as a translator/writer/copy editor to companies requiring material in English?

● Is there a need for child-minders?

● Could your cooking skills be put to good use in some way?

Finding out more
The ACCESS *Job Booklet* (see page 71) includes a complete chapter on self-employment, and much of the information is also included in their separate factsheet on *Starting Your Own Business*. Both take you through the whole procedure, step by step, explaining the various kinds of company which can be set up, from a one-man business to a public company. Other sections cover such subjects as finance and taxation, and there are lists of advisory bodies and other helpful agencies.

UK citizens should also contact their local tax office before leaving to find out more about their tax liability in the UK. The same office can also supply copies of relevant Inland Revenue publications, including *Residents and non-residents* (IR20) and *Living or Retiring Abroad?* (IR138). Libraries and Citizens' Advice Bureaus may also have copies of some Inland Revenue leaflets. They can also be obtained by post from PO Box 37, St Austell, Cornwall PL25 5YN, UK. Or you can telephone the order-line on 0845 9000404 between 8am and 10pm, seven days a week (except Christmas Day). In addition, many leaflets are available on the internet at www.inlandrevenue.gov.uk

US citizens can obtain a copy of the booklet *Tax Guide for United States Citizens Abroad* from any US embassy or consulate, or from an Internal Revenue Service office in the United States.

CASE STUDIES

Susan finds an opening

Once I'd decided I was going to try and live here, I found out all I could about work prospects and also started learning Dutch. Then I contacted every hospital, writing my application in Dutch to show that I could speak quite a bit of the langauge. It worked. Eventually, someone wrote back and suggested I contact them after my arrival. So I took a chance and made the move.

Ian hopes for the best

I just wanted to spend a year or two abroad between college and embarking on a proper career. I liked Holland, so I decided to give it a try. Thanks to all the hints from friends I made here, I've managed to keep my head above water. But I think it would be very different if I was looking for a long-term career.

Diane becomes self-employed

When I first came here, I worked full time for a company that produced a lot of English-language publications. But I left after I had my second child. After my divorce, I wanted to get back into full-time employment, but found my options very limited. I speak good Dutch, but it's still a barrier. I have managed to get a little freelance work from my previous employers, and occasionally from other publishers. But it's not enough for a family of three to live on.

CHECKLIST

1. Have you discovered whether your qualifications will be recognised in the Netherlands?

2. Have you considered all the work possibilities, and contacted everyone who could possibly help you in your search?

3. Could you start your own business?

directory. The social security agencies (*GUO, SFB, CADANS, GAK Nederland bv* and *USZO*) are responsible for benefits falling under the *WAZ, WAO, WW, ZW* and *TW*. Your employer will be able to give you the name and address of the relevant agency.

The *ABW* is covered by Municipal Social Services. You'll find them in your local telephone directory, under *Gemeente instellingen – dienst sociale zaken.*

Finding out more

A leaflet, *A short survey of social security in the Netherlands,* is available from the Ministry of Social Affairs and Employment (*Ministerie van Sociale Zaken en Werkgelegenheid*). It lists the various schemes in operation and the contributions payable.

* Ministerie van Sociale Zaken en Werkgelegenheid, Directie Voorlichting, Postbus 90801, 2509 LV Den Haag, The Netherlands.

DISCOVERING THE RIGHTS OF EU NATIONALS

The UK Benefits Agency publishes a booklet entitled *Going Abroad and Social Security Benefits* (GL29), which outlines the general rules for those going abroad. In addition its booklet *Your social security insurance, benefits and health care rights in the European Community, and in Iceland, Liechtenstein and Norway* (SA29) contains information specific to the EEA (European Economic Area), which includes all European Community countries. Both are available from the agency itself.

* The Benefits Agency, Pensions and Overseas Benefits Directorate, Department of Social Security, Tyneview Park, Benton, Newcastle upon Tyne NE98 1BA, UK. Tel: (0191) 218 7777. Fax (0191) 218 7293.

Additional information is available from your nearest Social Security office in the UK.

Transferring benefits

If you are receiving any kind of benefit, you should contact your local Social Security office **before you leave** to find out whether or not your benefit will continue to be paid.

Drawing sickness benefit

If you receive sickness benefit in the UK, for instance, you may be able to transfer payment to the Netherlands. But you should contact your local DSS office for further information before leaving.

Obtaining unemployment benefit
Jobseeker's Allowance is paid only under certain conditions and for a limited period of time while you are looking for work in another EU state. Unemployed people often lose their right to benefits because they leave the country of their last employment without registering with its un-employment services. Or they leave it too late before they register with the employment services of the state where they are hoping to find work. Or they stay for longer than the three months' job-seeking period permitted.

So you should make a point of contacting the UK office which pays your unemployment benefit well before you are planning to leave. They will tell you all you need to know, and also give you a form E303 which you will need to present at the Employment Office *(Arbeidsbureau)* in the Netherlands if you are to receive any benefit without undue delay.

Transferring pensions
For further information on pensions, contact the Overseas Benefits depart-ment of the DSS Benefits Agency, at the address given above.

Special regulations for self-employed EU citizens
If you are normally self-employed in the UK it is possible for you to carry on being insured under the UK National Insurance scheme as long as you do not expect to remain in the Netherlands for more than 12 months – and provided that you satisfy certain criteria. You will not then have to pay Dutch social security contributions.

Further information can be obtained from the Contributions Agency of the DSS.

● The Contributions Agency, International Services, Department of Social Security, Longbenton, Newcastle upon Tyne NE98 1YX, UK. Tel: (0191) 225 4811. Fax: (0191) 225 7800.

ORGANISING SUITABLE HEALTH INSURANCE

UK nationals who remain insured under the UK National Insurance scheme can obtain urgent medical treatment free of charge in the Netherlands pro-vided they are in possession of form E111, obtainable from any post office in the UK. But, even if you are covered by this form, you should still take out private insurance to cover any non-emergency treatment.

Visiting the dentist *(tandarts)*

Again, your *ziekenfonds* will be able to tell you the names of those who offer treatment under the fund. The services covered by a health insurance fund are very limited, but you can take out additional insurance to cover other treatment such as crowns.

If you are not with a *ziekenfonds,* you will have to take out private insurance, or pay for any treatment yourself. Friends or colleagues should be able to recommend a practitioner to you.

Check the wording on any insurance policy carefully, however. You could find that it is invalidated if you don't have regular check-ups.

You may also want to check that your chosen dentist usually provides anaesthetics. Most younger ones now do. But you could still find that some do not – and you may have to pay, even if you are covered by a *ziekenfonds.*

Having a baby

Natural childbirth is the norm in the Netherlands and the majority of babies are now born at home with a midwife *(verloskundige)* in attendance. Those who opt for hospital delivery normally return home within a few hours.

If there are no medical indications for a hospital delivery, you will probably have to cover the costs yourself. With a home delivery, you may also have to contribute, although your contribution may only be a small one. Your *ziekenfonds* or insurance company will be able to tell you more.

It is also worth enquiring about home maternity services *(kraamzorg-verenigingen).* They can provide a maternity assistant *(kraamverzorgster)* for eight days following delivery – to take care of other children, look after the house and provide further invaluable help to the new mother. But you will have to register with such a service before the end of the third month of pregnancy. Your *ziekenfonds* or insurance company will tell you how much they will contribute towards the cost.

You must register the birth at your town hall within three days.

Learning some useful words and phrases

Most of those working in the medical field have some knowledge of English. But it can still be comforting to have a few basic words and phrases at your fingertips. If you have a **pre-existing condition,** for instance, find out the Dutch word for it.

The following may also be useful:

blood pressure	*bloeddruk*
cold	*verkoudheid*
constipation	*(darm) verstopping*
cough	*hoest*

diarrhoea	*diarree*
(to) faint	*flauwvallen*
fever	*koorts*
flu	*griep*
headache	*hoofdpijn*
infection	*ontsteking*
miscarriage	*miskraam*
nauseous	*misselijk*
pain	*pijn*
pregnant	*zwanger*
prescription	*recept*
rash	*uitslag*
sore throat	*keelpijn*
stomach ache	*maagpijn*
toothache	*kiespijn*
(to) vomit	*overgeven*
unconscious	*bewusteloos*

Finding further information
ACCESS publish a detailed guide to health care in the Netherlands. Copies can be purchased direct from them.

● ACCESS, Plein 24, 2511 CS Den Haag, The Netherlands. Tel: (070) 346 2525. Fax (070) 356 1332.

CASE STUDIES

Susan discovers her rights
The first time I received a payslip here, it was totally incomprehensible, even though I already spoke quite a bit of Dutch. And even my Dutch boyfriend couldn't tell me what it all meant. So I was pleased to discover there is an explanatory booklet in English. I feel more secure knowing what my rights are, and where I should apply if I ever need any benefits.

Ian pays for his mistake
I thought I would be able to draw unemployment benefit here while I looked for work. But I never thought about making enquiries before I left. I'd intended to take my time finding work here. But I ended up having to take the first thing I was offered. Otherwise I could have ended up having to go back home.

Kay has a baby
My youngest child was born here, and it was very different from the birth

list of English-speaking schools. Write to any in the area where you plan to live, and ask for a copy of their prospectus and details of their entrance requirements and fees. Most produce illustrated brochures detailing their facilities and the academic programme followed.

The Foundation for International Education (*Stichting Internationaal Onderwijs*) carries school-by-school details on its website at www.sio.nl. The information includes age range, type of education, type of qualification, admission requirements and fees.

● Stichting Internationaal Onderwijs, c/o Mr H L F 's-Gravesande, Postbus 12.652, 2500 DP Den Haag, The Netherlands. Tel: (070) 353 2659.

The European Council of International Schools (ECIS) can also provide a list of their members in the Netherlands and publishes a directory of ECIS International Schools around the world.

● European Council of International Schools, 21 Lavant Street, Petersfield, Hampshire GU32 3EL, UK. Tel: (01730) 268244. Fax: (01730) 267914.

ACCESS, the information service for English speakers, can also provide information on Dutch schools.

● ACCESS, Plein 24, 2511 CS Den Haag, The Netherlands. Tel: (070) 346 2525. Fax: (070) 356 1332.

ATTENDING A DUTCH SCHOOL

Full-time education in the Netherlands is **compulsory** from the age of five to the end of the school year in which the child reaches the age of 16.

However, most children start school from the age of four, and part-time education must continue until they are 18.

Children attend a primary school for the first eight years, going on to secondary education at the age of 12. Secondary education can last four, five or six years.

Finding a primary school

You will need to choose a school and enrol your child before his fifth birthday. You'll find one in most towns and villages, but you don't have to choose the one nearest to where you live.

Go and look at some local schools, and talk to teachers there. Don't worry if you don't speak Dutch. Most teachers will speak good English.

And if they don't, you'll have to decide whether that is the best school for a child that may not yet speak Dutch.

Some schools provide extra help for those who don't speak Dutch. Some schools may have extra lessons teaching the language and culture of your native country. There are also special schools for those unable to attend a normal school due to illness, disability or learning difficulties.

Talk to friends, neighbours and colleagues with children, too. Their insight could be invaluable. The subjects taught are set down by law, but teaching methods may vary considerably. Facilities must be provided for those who want to stay at school during the lunch break. But in general the costs involved are passed on to the parents, and children need to take their own packed lunch.

Paying for primary education
At primary level, education is almost always paid for by the government – including text books and exercise books. But you may be asked to contribute towards the cost of special activities like outings and sports days.

Choosing a secondary school
During your child's eighth year at primary school, you will have to make a decision about a secondary school. Your choice will depend on both how well your child is doing and what they want to be when they grow up. Your child's present teachers will be able to help.

You may find that your child has to take an examination before leaving the primary school, to test the skills learnt there.

A number of different types of secondary education is available:

- HAVO = senior general secondary education
- VWO = pre-university education
- VMBO = pre-vocational secondary education.

An extremely informative guide on *Going to School in the Netherlands* explains what each entails. It is available in English and a number of other languages, at no charge.

- DOP, Postbus 20014, 2500 AN Den Haag, The Netherlands.

Parents can choose their child's secondary school. But it is up to the school itself to decide whether the child is admitted. The advice of the primary school will be taken into consideration, and many primary schools use a leaving examination to assess the level the pupils have reached.

Again, you may have several suitable schools in your area, and it is a

Diane's children receive a Dutch education

My children were born here and I always expected that we would stay here. So they go to regular Dutch schools. They are bi-lingual, because we've always spoken English at home and Dutch outside the house. But their qualifications will be Dutch ones. I did think of returning to England after my divorce. But I was worried about them starting over again in a totally different system. And in any case, neither of them wanted to leave. Holland is their home.

CHECKLIST

1. Are you looking for short-term or long-term schooling for your children?

2. What kind of education would be most useful to them and what kind of school would provide it?

3. Are there any opportunities for you to further your own education?

10

Everyday Living in the Netherlands

SHOPPING

With some English spoken almost everywhere, and no one expecting foreign visitors to master even the most basic of Dutch phrases, shopping in Holland is far less traumatic than in many other European countries. But outside the major tourist areas – where a high level of proficiency in English, German and possibly French or Spanish is often a prerequisite for a job as a shop assistant – communication can still be difficult. Not because shopkeepers are unwilling to help, but simply because they may lack the vocabulary to understand your needs. It is therefore worth trying to learn at least a few relevant words.

Opening hours

Most shops are open from 9.00 or 9.30 am until 6.00 pm, with late-night shopping until 9.00 pm on one day each week (*koopavond*) – usually Thursday or Friday. But in many cases they are closed on Monday mornings.

Shops are also usually closed on Sundays, but in an increasing number of towns they now open on the first Sunday of the month. In some places you may find them closed on Wednesday afternoons.

Finding the necessities

If your local shop assistants speak little English, you may find it easier at first to shop in a supermarket, such as Albert Heijn, Edah or Aldi. In a supermarket, you can pick out vegetables without knowing their Dutch names. You'll see which cuts of meat look reasonably similar to those bought at home. You can spot familiar brand names, however different the Dutch pronunciation. And you can buy a packet of tasty-looking biscuits, whatever strange name they have been given.

Above all, supermarket shopping encourages you to try out all sorts of tempting new foods that you would not otherwise know existed – and you won't even have to open your mouth. Figure 9, however, gives translations for some of the items you may wish to add to your shopping list.

One word of warning, however. If the cashier says something you don't

Basics

butter	*boter*
bread	*brood*
coffee	*koffie*
cream	*room*
eggs	*eieren*
flour	*bloem*
milk	*melk*
low fat	*halfvolle melk*
skimmed	*magere melk*
whole fat	*volle melk*
rice	*rijst*
sugar	*zuiker*
tea	*thee*

Fruit and vegetables

apple	*appel*
banana	*banaan*
cabbage	*kool*
carrot	*worteltje/peintje*
cauliflower	*bloemkool*
celery	*bleekselderij*
cherries	*kersen*
chicory	*witlof*
cucumber	*komkommer*
garlic	*knoflook*
grapes	*druiven*
lemon	*citroen*
lettuce	*sla*
mushrooms	*champignons*
onion	*ui*
orange	*sinaasappel*
peach	*perzik*
peas	*ertwen*
pineapple	*ananas*
potato	*aardappel*
raspberries	*frambozen*
strawberries	*aardbeien*
tomato	*tomaat*

Meat

beef	*rundvlees*
lamb	*lamsvlees*
pork	*varkensvlees*
sausage	*worst*
veal	*kalfsvlees*

Fish

cod	*kabeljauw*
crab	*krab*
eel	*paling*
haddock	*schelvis*
herring	*haring*
mackerel	*makreel*
plaice	*schol*
salmon	*zalm*
shrimps	*garnalen*
sole	*tong*
tuna	*tonijn*

Herbs and spices

bayleaf	*laurierblad*
chives	*bieslook*
cinnamon	*kaneel*
cloves	*kruidnagelen*
curry powder	*kerriepoeder*
nutmeg	*nootmuskaat*
parsley	*peterselie*
pepper	*peper*
sage	*salie*
salt	*zout*

Fig. 9. A food shopping list.

understand, don't be tempted just to smile and nod. She may be saying *'Zegels?'* In other words, she is asking whether you want savings stamps. Some are free, but not all. So you could find the additional charge added to your bill – and the stamps can only be redeemed (albeit at a profit) when a sizable number have been gathered.

Weighing it up

Many goods can be bought by the Dutch pound *(pond),* which is half a kilo-gramme or 500 grams (a bit more than an Imperial lb). So a *half pond* is 250 grams, or a little more than half a pound.

An *ons* is 100 grams. So although 100 grams may sound like an ounce, it is actually quite different. *Twee* (two) *ons* is 200 grams, *drie* (three) *ons* is 300 grams and so on. *Anderhalf ons* is 150 grams.

Buying bread

Even supermarkets often have personal service at their bakery counters, and it's worth learning the few words needed to obtain what you require.

Freshly baked loaves, for instance, are normally displayed on shelves, so all you have to do is point to the one required. But if all that matters to you is whether it is white or brown, simply ask for *wittebrood* or *bruinbrood* respectively. Wholewheat is *volkoren.*

You can buy a whole loaf *(heel)* or a half *(half).* And most loaves can also be sliced for you – just ask for *gesneden.* Rolls are *broodjes* and French sticks are *stokbrood.*

Look out for a *warme bakker* (literally 'hot baker'), either in your super-market or a separate specialist shop. That means that bread is baked on the premises, and you may even find that your loaf is still warm when you get it home. A *banketbakkerij,* on the other hand, is a cake shop, and the two do not necessarily go together.

Don't just say cheese

Many types of cheese are on sale in Holland, but the most common type of Dutch cheese is that made in Gouda. And the older it is, the stronger its taste.

The youngest of all is *roomkaas,* a deliciously creamy cheese, as its name suggests. *Jong* is a little older, but still very mild. *Belegen* is medium-mature, with a stronger flavour, while *oud* is the most mature of all, with a crumbly texture and powerful aroma. As if that weren't enough, there is also *jong belegen,* which is somewhere between *jong* and *belegen,* and *oud belegen,* which is rather more mature than ordinary *belegen.*

The good thing is that any specialist cheese seller *(kaasboer),* in a shop or on a market stall, will allow you to taste a morsel before buying. So you can try out several before making up your mind. Cheese can also be sliced for you. Ask for it *in plakjes.*

Buying clothes

The European system of sizing is very different from both the English and the American systems. You'll find some (very approximate) equivalents given in Figure 10. But you'll find clothes on sale from all over Europe, and this means enormous variations in sizing and fit. The only solution is to keep trying things on, and eventually you'll probably find that many of your purchases come from a limited number of chains.

Women's clothing

Dutch	36	38	40	42	44	46
English	10	12	14	16	18	20
US	8	10	12	14	16	18

Men's shirts

Dutch	36	37	38	39	40	41
English	14	$14^1/_2$	15	$15^1/_2$	16	$16^1/_2$

Men's suits and knitwear

Dutch		44	46	48	50	52	54
English/US		34	36	38	40	42	44

Fig. 10. Clothing sizes.

FINDING ENGLISH-LANGUAGE BOOKS AND PERIODICALS

Many Dutch newsagents will sell some English-language newspapers and magazines, especially in major cities. Bookshops, too, will often have an English-language section. But in Amsterdam and The Hague you'll also find some shops specialising entirely in English and American books.

There are also various periodicals for expatriates, which can provide invaluable information, especially for the newcomer. The monthly *Roundabout*, for instance, includes a comprehensive list of events, while *Expat at Home* offers both interesting articles and useful relocation information.

● *Roundabout*, Postbus 96813, 2509 JE Den Haag, The Netherlands. Tel: (070) 324 1611.

● *Expat at Home*, Postbus 17427, 1001 JK Amsterdam, The Netherlands. Tel: (020) 620 8517.

COOKING AND EATING THE DUTCH WAY

Breakfast
You won't find cooked breakfasts in any Dutch household. At most, you'll be offered a boiled egg – and even that may not be hot. But this doesn't mean that the Dutch skimp on their first meal of the day. Far from it.

A traditional Dutch breakfast consists of slices of bread with a variety of savoury or sweet toppings. There may be a choice of cheeses and two or three kinds of sliced meat, as well as various preserves, and perhaps several different kinds of *hagelslag* – sweet strands or flakes (often chocolate ones), similar to those used as cake decorations in other countries.

You could find two or three different kinds of bread, including the darkest of rye bread or *roggebrood*. And everything, whether sweet or savoury, is eaten with a knife and fork.

A tin of Dutch rusks, or *beschuit,* might also be found on the table, to be spread with butter and then topped with cheese or jam or *hagelslag.* Currant bread, or *krentenbrood,* is eaten with cheese. And slices of heavily spiced *ontbijtkoek,* or breakfast cake, may be served on their own or spread with butter.

Most important of all is the pot of strong coffee, served with the thick evaporated milk known as *koffiemelk* (unless you ask for it black).

Lunch
With lunch breaks often short, office workers will probably grab a roll or some kind of hot or cold snack from a takeaway or the company canteen. But if you are visiting, you may be given a meal similar to breakfast, but more elaborate. The more festive the occasion, the wider will be the choice of breads and rolls, and of cheeses and cold meats. And once again, the whole is often washed down with coffee, which is why such a meal is known as a *koffietafel,* or coffee table.

Other popular lunch-time dishes include soup, often eaten with huge spoons that would be used as serving spoons in other countries. Pea soup is a favourite in winter, made so thick that the spoon will almost stand up in it.

Huzarensalade (hussar salad), on the other hand, is a chilled mixture of potatoes, meat and vegetables bound with mayonnaise. Another popular midday meal is the *uitsmijter* – literally the 'throwing outer', since these were once served at the end of parties to indicate that it was time to go home. Two slices of bread are topped with cheese or sliced meat (usually ham or roast beef) and two fried eggs.

Preparing dinner

These days the majority of Dutch people keep their main meal for the evening. That is when they will usually indulge in *warme eten* (hot food). You'll find restaurants catering for every taste and offering food from all over the globe. But in Dutch homes you'll generally find rather simpler fare, except on special occasions.

Ovens are now increasingly used, but some homes still do not have one. Instead, the cooker may consist of four gas burners, perhaps sitting on top of a fridge. So meat will often be fried or braised, rather than grilled or roasted.

Potatoes are a major part of most meals, and are cooked in a special way. After boiling, they are drained and then returned to a low heat to dry them, so that the outsides become crumbly. The pan must be shaken frequently to make sure that they don't burn.

Desserts are generally light and simple. A carton of yogurt, perhaps, or some *vla* (custard, served chilled), or perhaps some ice cream.

Keeping out the cold

Traditional Dutch foods tend to be hearty, like the famous *winterschotels* or winter dishes.

Boerenkool is a mixture of curly kale and mashed potatoes and is usually served with *rookworst,* a smoked sausage widely available in easy boil-in-the-bag packaging. *Hutspot* mixes carrots and onions with mashed potatoes, and is traditionally eaten with *klapstuk,* a kind of stewed beef. *Zuurkool,* or sauerkraut, is likewise often mixed with mashed potatoes, while a rather different winter offering is made with *capucijners,* or marrowfat peas.

Trying some other Dutch specialities

Pancakes may be either sweet (topped with syrup, or *stroop,* perhaps) or savoury, and are often served as a complete meal. But those with smaller appetites may prefer the mini *poffertjes* – tiny pancakes that will be made while you watch. They are served with a dollop of butter and a sprinkling of castor sugar plus, if you wish, any one of a whole variety of liqueurs.

Other favourite snacks include *saté* – small pieces of pork, chicken or goat grilled on sticks and then covered with a spicy peanut butter sauce (*pindasaus*). *Pindasaus* is also used on chips (*patates),* although they are traditionally served with a thick mayonnaise. And *pindasaus* crops up again in some of the dishes that make up an Indonesian *rijsttafel.*

Discovering Indonesian food

A good Indonesian *rijsttafel* will consist of at least a dozen small meat and vegetable dishes – and often many more – ranging from mild to extremely hot and spicy, and served with boiled and fried rice. But beware the innocent-looking sambals, served in separate small dishes. A tiny knife-tip helping will take the roof of your mouth off.

Virtually every small town and village will have at least one Chinese-Indonesian restaurant. Any *rijsttafel* on sale here will probably be adapted for the Dutch palate. For a real one you need a proper Indonesian restaurant.

But that doesn't mean you should avoid your local Chinese-Indonesian. They will also usually sell takeaways, with huge portions of *nasi goreng* and *nasi rames* for just a few guilders – often more than enough for two. The former is a mixture of fried rice with meat and vegetables, and may be topped with a slice or two of cold meat and a fried egg. The latter contains many of the dishes from the *rijsttafel*, but on a single plate and at a fraction of the price.

Expect long queues on a Sunday, however. Traditionally, it is the day Dutch housewives are given time off from cooking. So the restaurant will be packed with hungry Dutch families, and with husbands and children ordering food to take home.

Tasting the national dish

Holland's national dish is herring, eaten raw and available from many a roadside stall. The traditional way to eat the fish is to hold it up by its tail, throw your head back and dangle the herring above your face, trying to catch it in your mouth. But these days it is often cut into pieces for you and served on a small dish. Pieces are speared with a cocktail stick and may be dipped in raw chopped onions before being transferred to the mouth.

FINDING A TASTE OF HOME

It is possible to re-create many favourite dishes from ingredients you will find in your local shops. But sometimes they are simply not quite the same, and you may find yourself longing for a taste of home. Delicatessens often offer a wide variety of canned and packaged foods from other countries. But you'll find a particularly good selection in cities like Amsterdam and The Hague.

If you are from the UK, however, you'll also find increasing numbers of familiar products in your local supermarket. And fellow expats may also be able to tell you how to adapt your favourite recipes using the ingredients available to you.

CASE STUDIES

Susan learns to cook again

When Karel and I first moved in together, one of the most difficult things for me was learning to cook in the Dutch way. The cuts of meat were different, because of the way it's cooked here. And even simple things like boiling potatoes suddenly had to be re-learnt. I finally persuaded a Dutch friend to give me some basic lessons. In return, I taught her how to make a few simple cakes, which she finds really impresses her mother-in-law!

Ian gets by

I'm lucky, really, living in Amsterdam, as everyone speaks at least some English. Most of the shops round here are small, family-run businesses, though, and you often have to explain what you want. It's not out on display. But I can usually manage to get by with a mixture of English and sign language.

Often, though, I eat at a snack bar or something. I'm not a good cook and the choice of ready meals over here is pretty limited – especially if you don't have an oven. Anyway, I can't always make out the instructions.

Kay shops for the flavours of home

I spent a lot of time searching out ingredients to make the family's favourite dishes, and there were some terrible disasters at first. But I've discovered alternatives to most things now, and I stock up on others during our annual trips home. I know I should perhaps have learnt to cook in the Dutch way. But most of our friends seem to enjoy the American dishes. Fellow Americans appreciate a taste of home, and any Dutch visitors seem to like the novelty of something foreign.

Diane enjoys the best of both worlds

Over the years, I suppose you could say that my lifestyle has really become Anglo-Dutch. I used to buy all my clothes in England, for instance. Now, I just pick up the odd item on visits to my family.

My cooking is a real mixture of Dutch dishes and English ones. I serve coffee in the Dutch way, with thick and creamy *koffiemelk*. But I do still enjoy a good English cup of tea, and buy huge quantities if I'm in the UK.

I still buy stacks of English magazines and books whenever I'm back in England as well. They are expensive here, and I just don't enjoy the Dutch ones so much.

CHECKLIST

1. Do you know what times your local shops open?

2. Do you know your Dutch clothes sizes?

3. How adventurous are you prepared to be when it comes to shopping and cooking?

11

Socialising and Special Occasions

MAKING VISITORS WELCOME

The Dutch set great store by hospitality, and whenever you enter a Dutch home, or even an office, you can expect to be offered at least something to drink, and very often more. You will be expected to do the same when people visit you.

Daytime entertaining

During the morning, you should offer coffee to anyone who calls – preferably good, strong **filter coffee** rather than the instant variety. Unless someone asks for black, you should add a small helping of *koffiemelk*, the thick evaporated milk that the Dutch use in their white coffee. If you don't know how much to use, simply put it on the table in a little jug, alongside the sugar.

A biscuit would probably be welcome, too, but you needn't add anything more elaborate than that.

Many people drink coffee in the afternoon as well. But you should also offer the alternative of **tea** – served weak and black, rather than with milk. If you ever ask for milk for your tea (especially in a restaurant), you will probably be given *koffiemelk*, which will soon wean you off the habit.

You might like to offer **cake** with the afternoon tea or coffee. But if you ask for 'cake' in a Dutch bakery, you'll be given something like a plain madeira cake. Fancy cakes and gateaux are known as *gebak*.

Later on in the afternoon, say after 5.00 pm, it's normal to offer a **drink** or *borrel*. But you don't need to provide a wide choice. Most men will be happy with a *genever*, or Dutch gin, and women with wine or sherry, although it's also a good idea to have some orange juice available for those who don't want alcohol.

On warm days, it's also usual to offer the alternative of something *fris* or fresh in place of the tea or coffee. This could again be orange juice, or one of the fizzy drinks that the Dutch consume in vast quantities.

Evening entertaining

Evening visitors would again be offered coffee – perhaps with a *gebak* if you want to be really welcoming. Later you would move on to other beverages. But again you don't need to offer a wide choice. Beer, wine, *genever* and something *fris* would be choice enough. It's worth keeping a small stock of crisps and other savoury snacks to offer on such occasions, too. And cubes of cheese also go down well when dinner is already some hours away.

VISITING SOMEONE'S HOME

If you have been given a specific time, you should try to arrive punctually, even if the invitation is simply for a cup of coffee. Don't think it is fashionable to arrive late. It will simply be considered bad manners.

Say it with flowers

If you are visiting a Dutch home for anything more elaborate than a cup of coffee, you should not arrive empty-handed. The gift need not be elaborate. A couple of beautifully packaged chocolates would always go down well. Or do what most Dutch people do and say it with flowers.

You don't need to buy an elaborate bunch unless it's a really special occasion. In fact, your hostess will probably be exceedingly embarrassed to receive a giant bouquet when all she is offering you is tea and cake. But you can't go wrong with a small bunch of blooms bought for a few guilders from any flower stall.

The Dutch also use flowers where those in other countries might use cards – to say thank you, or happy birthday, or congratulations on an engagement or exam success.

Greeting the other guests

Once you've greeted your hostess and parted with your flowers, don't forget to shake hands with anyone else present before you sit down. If they are total strangers, you don't need to wait to be introduced. Just smile and say your name as you shake hands, and they will do likewise.

A man and woman who are old friends might, on the other hand, greet each other with a kiss on both cheeks (and, if they are really close, perhaps with a third peck on the cheek they kissed first). A woman might also greet a close woman friend with a kiss on each cheek. But male friends would shake hands.

CELEBRATING BIRTHDAYS

Birthdays are major events in the Netherlands, so don't expect yours to go unmarked. At the office, even the boss is likely to shake you warmly by the hand and wish you *hartelijk gefeliciteerd* (congratulations). What's more, it is not only your own birthday that brings about such treatment. Mention that a sibling, parent or spouse is celebrating theirs, and you can expect a stream of congratulatory handshakes from colleagues.

If you are the one with the birthday, you can also expect to spend the evening holding open house for family and friends. Unless you tell people that you have other plans, a string of callers will make their way to your door after dinner – each one bringing flowers and/or other gifts, and expecting some hospitality in return.

If you're a woman, you may therefore spend your birthday evening in the kitchen, serving up drinks and tasty snacks and emerging only to welcome each new visitor. Men, of course, send their wives to the kitchen and sit back to enjoy all the attention. Little wonder, then, that a few women are now choosing other means of celebrating.

Even so, it probably won't be long before you receive an invitation to such a birthday gathering, and it certainly helps to know the ropes.

Bearing gifts

You should never turn up without at least a token gift, however distant an acquaintance the birthday person. Once again, you cannot go wrong with cut flowers, fitting the size of the bunch to the closeness of the friendship and the importance of the occasion.

House plants are often even more welcome, however, as every Dutch home has windowsills crammed with foliage of all kinds. But don't make the mistake of turning up with a simple terracotta flowerpot, however elaborate the blooms. Look on any Dutch sill, and you'll see that every pot is tastefully encased in something more decorative. You should find a selection on sale alongside the plants themselves, usually at very reasonable prices.

For closer friends, you might also like to take another gift. But it's usual to take flowers as well, even if it is just a token bunch.

Arriving at the party

Once you've parted with your gifts, you then start the complicated round of 'congratulations' – not just of the person whose birthday it is but also of any husband/wife, children, parents and even sometimes the closest of the friends who happen to be present.

As you go round the room shaking hands with those present, and introducing yourself to strangers, you have to remember that other people might need to be congratulated, too. What's more, Jan Meyer might not tell you (or anyone else) that he is Anneke Haarsma's brother. When the light dawns hours later, as conversation turns to childhood memories, everyone then has to leap up to shake hands again and proffer the missing congratulations.

Again, you may be offered coffee and *gebak* before moving on to something stronger. But these days, many birthday gatherings start very late in the evening (possibly as late as 10.00 pm). In that case, you would expect to miss out the coffee stage altogether.

A succession of savoury snacks will probably be offered with the alcoholic drinks. But you should not take one until they are offered to you, or until you are asked to help yourself.

If you are later offered more coffee (perhaps with a filled roll), this is an indication that it is time to leave.

ATTENDING A WEDDING

Dutch weddings can be something of a marathon, both for the couple themselves and for some of the guests. A civil ceremony at the town hall may be followed by a church service. If it's a morning wedding, there may be a lunch for close family and friends, and perhaps some kind of reception to fill the afternoon. And then in the evening the main party begins, with an endless succession of tasty *hapjes* or snacks and a constant refilling of empty glasses.

Your invitation should make it clear which elements you are invited to attend. But in general the official ceremonies and daytime receptions are reserved for family and the closest of friends, with everyone else being invited to join in the evening revels.

Drinks usually flow freely. But when coffee and rolls are brought round, it is once again a signal to leave.

CELEBRATING THE TWO-TIER CHRISTMAS

Remembering St Nicholas

It is not Christmas but St Nicholas Eve, 20 days earlier, which is eagerly awaited by children in Holland. The benevolent saint was born in Asia Minor in 271 AD. But legend now has him hailing from Spain, from whence he apparently travels to Amsterdam towards the end of November, together with his Moorish page Peter.

After his triumphant entry into the city, the Sinterklaas season has officially begun. From then on, children expectantly leave out a shoe at night, perhaps with a carrot or some hay as a gift for the saint's horse. In the morning, if the child has been good, the offering has gone and in its place the child finds a small gift or sweet.

It could be a spicey *speculaas* biscuit (often made in the shape of a windmill), or some sugary fondant sweets.

The main exchange of gifts, however, is on the evening of 5 December, or *Sinterklaasavond* (St Nicholas Eve) – the evening before the anniversary of the saint's death, which is his official saint's day. It is mainly an evening for children, and today many adults don't bother to celebrate it at all. But children look forward to it for weeks.

Celebrating Christmas

More and more families are now starting to exchange gifts on Christmas Day rather than at St Nicholas – a move which has not met with the approval of the more traditionally minded. But the highlight of the day will usually be a special meal, which could be turkey or goose but could just as easily be anything else that the family fancy.

Many families will eat out on either Christmas Day or Boxing Day, so if you plan to do the same you will need to book early.

Christmas trees start to go up as soon as St Nicholas is over – often at least partially decorated with chocolate ornaments or fondant *kerstkransjes*. And there will almost certainly be lots of candles. (The sounds of sirens are common at this time of year, as the fire brigade attends yet another burning tree.)

OTHER ANNUAL FESTIVALS

Bringing in the New Year

Unless you are living way out in the country, you will not be given the chance to ignore New Year's Eve in Holland. In many ways, it is the most festive occasion of the year, with parties and family gatherings organised to mark the occasion.

Oliebollen, deep fried doughnuts, are traditionally served along with the drinks and other party snacks in the run-up to midnight. Then, on the stroke of twelve, the whole country erupts in a riot of fireworks. There is much hand shaking and kissing on both cheeks and wishing of a happy new year, and phones start to ring as distant friends and relatives try to be the first with their good wishes. Some families even follow all this with a sumptuous banquet in the early hours, washed down with champagne saved for the occasion.

Sleep is impossible for at least the first two hours of the new year, and there may be sporadic explosions even further into the night as revellers try to prolong the festivities.

Luckily, the following day is a holiday. But there is much more shaking of hands and wishing of happy new year when offices reopen after the break.

Observing the Queen's official birthday

A very different kind of celebration is on *Koninginnedag*, or the Queen's official birthday, on 30 April. It's actually the birthday of the previous

Queen, Juliana, mother of the present Queen Beatrix. But as Beatrix was born on 31 January, at the coldest and most miserable time of the year, she opted to keep *Koninginnedag* where it was, so that people could continue to celebrate it with carnivals and fairs as they had done before.

Dutch flags fly from many houses, often together with an orange pennant representing the House of Orange. Hordes of people also take to the streets. On *Koninginnedag*, private individuals can trade freely, and many will set up a stand on the street to sell all sorts of unwanted household goods. Children sell toys they have grown out of. Buskers abound, and cities like Amsterdam are turned into a mammoth fleamarket frequented by crowds of browsers hoping to find a bargain. The festivities in many towns now begin on the previous evening – so it's worth checking if you're hoping for a bargain.

More annual fixtures

Easter Monday (*Tweede Paasdag*) is another public holiday, and many offices now offer staff a holiday on Good Friday (*Goede Vrijdag*) too, making Easter (or *Pasen*) an extra-long weekend. Nearly six weeks later, Ascension Day (or *Hemelvaartsdag*) provides another holiday (on a Thursday) and exactly seven weeks after Easter comes Whitsun (or *Pinksteren*), with another holiday Monday giving a long weekend.

MEETING FELLOW EXPATRIATES

However much you enjoy the Dutch way of life, however, it is still important to keep in touch with people from your own country. Not only can they provide moral support when homesickness strikes. They may also be able to offer up-to-date information when your residence permit needs renewing, or tell you about companies looking for English-speaking staff.

Joining a club

Your own country's embassy in the Netherlands will probably have a list of clubs and societies of particular interest to expatriates. The British embassy usually has a particularly comprehensive list.

● British Embassy, Lange Voorhout 10, 2514 ED Den Haag, The Netherlands. Tel: (070) 427 0427.

The British Society of Amsterdam
Founded in 1920, the British Society has a busy programme of activities, including sports of various kinds, coffee mornings, bridge and pub

evenings. A bonfire night and a Christmas party are also regular fixtures, and other events are organised according to the interests of members.

- British Society of Amsterdam, Postbus 7429, 1007 JK Amsterdam, The Netherlands.

The American Women's Club
The American Women's Club in The Hague has been running for nearly as long, and again has a busy programme of activities.

- American Women's Club, Nieuwe Duinweg 25, 2587 AB Den Haag, The Netherlands. Tel: (070) 350 6007.

The British Women's Club
The British Women's Club in The Hague has its own coffee shop and library, and organises talks, trips, sporting and other activities.

- British Women's Club, Sociëteit de Witte, Plein 24, 2511 CS Den Haag, The Netherlands. Tel: (070) 346 1973.

Australian and New Zealand Women's Club
Coffee mornings and lunches are among this club's activities, as well as evening events to which partners are invited.

- Australian and New Zealand Women's Club, c/o Mrs Carol Huysing, Van Zeggelenlaan 99, 2524 AC Den Haag, The Netherlands.

Netherlands England Society
The Netherlands England Society (*Genootschap Nederland Engeland*) has branches all over the Netherlands.

- Mrs Alida van Zon, Postbus 97834, 2509 GE Den Haag, The Netherlands. Tel: (079) 351 6127 or (071) 561 5209.

Further addresses
American Baseball Foundation. Tel: (070) 511 9067.
International Art Club, c/o Loes Verspoor, Landrestraat 989, 2551 BN Den Haag, The Netherlands.
Leiden English Speaking Theatre Group, Postbus 85, 2300 AB Leiden, The Netherlands. Tel: (071) 532 3704.
St Andrew's Society of the Netherlands, c/o Drusilla Wishart, Aert van Neslaan 221, 2341 HK Oegstgeest, The Netherlands.

Finding out what's on

Roundabout covers the whole country and includes an extensive day-by-day calendar of events.

- *Roundabout*, Postbus 96813, 2509 JE Den Haag, The Netherlands. Tel: (070) 324 1611.

CASE STUDIES

Susan attends some birthday parties

I used to find social occasions very confusing when I first came here. Especially birthdays. Karel comes from quite a large family, and they have all lived in this area all their lives. So there would be this sea of strange faces. Sometimes everyone would be congratulating me, and I had no idea why. Sometimes Karel would seem to be congratulating everyone in sight, whether it was their birthday or not.

My own birthday was the worst. Colleagues and patients kept coming up to me all day, shaking my hand and wishing me *hartelijk gefeliciteerd*, which seemed quite normal. But then I happened to mention how strange it was not to share my birthday with my twin, who was back home in England. Suddenly everyone leapt up and started shaking my hand all over again – to congratulate me on my sister's birthday.

Ian remains an outsider

I don't really know many Dutch people. Most of those I meet are foreigners like me, just here for a while before moving on. And I don't entertain much either. We tend to get together in bars or cafés and use our flats or rooms just as somewhere to sleep. As none of us has much in the way of furniture, it's more comfortable that way.

Kay entertains

When Jonathan was first moved here, it was an absolute nightmare. He was constantly bringing clients and colleagues home, and I always felt that I was doing the wrong thing.

Then I got to know the wife of one of the other ex pats. She's Dutch, but she understood how different some things were in Holland. I suppose you could say she took me under her wing.

Now it all seems easy. I make sure that I have a supply of crisps and other savoury snacks in the cupboard, along with bottles of *genever* and sherry, some beer and some orange juice. And I learnt to make a really good cup of coffee. That's very important.

Diane enjoys her social life

While I was married, I didn't really have much contact with other English-speaking people, and I think that was a mistake. I have lots of good Dutch friends, but they really couldn't understand how I could still sometimes feel homesick even after all these years.

I joined a couple of clubs after my divorce, and met up with a lot of other expatriates as a result. Now I have a large circle of British, American and Dutch friends. A lot of my social life revolves around my home and theirs, which suits me as I'm on a very tight budget. A bottle of wine isn't expensive. Add a few crisps or some cheese and you've all you need for an evening that's really *gezellig*, as they say here.

CHECKLIST

1.   What should you offer your visitors?

2.   What gift should you take when visiting?

3.   Are there any clubs or societies where you could meet up with others from your own country?

Useful Addresses

EMBASSIES

American Embassy, Lange Voorhout 102, 2514 EJ Den Haag, The Netherlands. Tel: (070) 310 9209.

British Embassy, Lange Voorhout 10, 2514 ED Den Haag, The Netherlands. Tel: (070) 427 0427.

Canadian Embassy, Sophialaan 7, 2514 KP Den Haag, The Netherlands. Tel: (070) 311 1600.

Embassy of Australia, Carnegielaan 4, 2517 KH Den Haag, The Netherlands. Tel: (070) 310 8200.

New Zealand Embassy, Carnegielaan 10, 2517 KH Den Haag, The Netherlands. Tel: (070) 346 9324.

Royal Netherlands Embassy, 38 Hyde Park Gate, London SW7 5DP, UK. Tel: (020) 7590 3200.

AU PAIRS

Activity International, Steentilstraat 25, 9711 GK Groningen, The Netherlands. Tel: (050) 313 0666.

CLUBS AND SOCIETIES

American Baseball Foundation. Tel: (070) 511 9067.

American Women's Club, Nieuwe Duinweg 25, 2587 AB Den Haag, The Netherlands. Tel: (070) 350 6007.

Australian and New Zealand Women's Club, c/o Mrs Carol Huysing, Van Zeggelenlaan 99, 2524 AC Den Haag, The Netherlands.

British Society of Amsterdam, Postbus 7429, 1007 JK Amsterdam, The Netherlands.

British Women's Club, Sociëteit de Witte, Plein 24, 2511 CS Den Haag, The Netherlands. Tel: (070) 346 1973.

International Art Club, c/o Loes Verspoor, Landrestraat 989, 2551 BN Den Haag, The Netherlands.

Leiden English Speaking Theatre Group, Postbus 85, 2300 AB Leiden, The

Netherlands. Tel: (071) 532 3704.

Netherlands England Society, Mrs Alida van Zon, Postbus 97834, 2509 GE Den Haag, The Netherlands. Tel: (079) 351 6127 or (071) 561 5209.

St Andrew's Society of the Netherlands, c/o Drusilla Wishart, Aert van Neslaan 221, 2341 HK Oegstgeest, The Netherlands.

EDUCATION

American School of The Hague, Rijksstraatweg 200, 2241 BX Wassenaar, The Netherlands. Tel: (070) 512 1060. Fax: (070) 511 2400.

The British School in the Netherlands, Rosenburgherlaan 2, 2252 BA Voorschoten, The Netherlands. Tel: (071) 561 6966.

British School of Amsterdam, Jan van Eijckstraat 21, 1077 LG Amsterdam, The Netherlands. Tel: (020) 679 7840. Fax: (020) 675 8396.

DOP, Postbus 20014, 2500 AN Den Haag, The Netherlands.

European Council of International Schools, 21 Lavant Street, Petersfield, Hampshire GU32 3EL, UK. Tel: (01730) 268244. Fax: (01730) 267914.

Foreign Student Service, Oranje Nassaulaan 5, 1075 AH Amsterdam, The Netherlands. Tel: (020) 671 5915.

The Foundation for International Education (Stichting Internationaal Onderwijs), c/o Mr H L F 's-Gravesande, Postbus 12.652, 2500 DP Den Haag, The Netherlands. Tel: (070) 353 2659.

International School of Amsterdam, Postbus 920, 1180 AX Amstelveen, The Netherlands. Tel: (020) 347 1111. Fax: (020) 347 1222.

International School The Hague, 75 Theo Mann Bouwmeesterlaan, 2597 GV Den Haag, The Netherlands. Tel: (070) 328 1450.

Joppenhof International Department, Kelvinstraat 3, 6227 VA Maastricht, The Netherlands. Tel: (043) 367 1335. Fax: (043) 367 2440.

Ministry of Education, Culture and Science (Ministerie van Onderwijs, Cultuur en Wetenschappen), Centrale Directie Voorlichting, Postbus 25000, 2700 LZ Zoetermeer, The Netherlands. Tel: (079) 323 4854.

Stichting Internationaal Onderwijs, Postbus 12.652, 2500 DP Den Haag, The Netherlands. Tel: (070) 353 2659.

LANGUAGE SCHOOLS

Amsterdam College, Dubbelink 3, 1102 AL Amsterdam ZO, The Netherlands. Tel: (020) 699 8078. Fax: (020) 600 2023.

Berlitz Schools of Language, Rokin 87-89, 1012 KL Amsterdam, The Netherlands. Tel: (020) 622 1375. Fax: (020) 620 3959.

The Berlitz School of Languages Limited, 9-13 Grosvenor Street, London W1A 3BZ, UK. Tel: (020) 7915 0909. Fax: (020) 7915 0222.

British Language Training Centre, Oxford House, N.Z. Voorburgwal 328E, 1012 RW Amsterdam, The Netherlands. Tel: (020) 622 3634. Fax: (020) 626 4962.

The British School in the Netherlands – International Education Centre, Vlaskamp 19, 2592 AA Den Haag, The Netherlands. Tel: (070) 333 8130. Fax: (070) 333 8132.

Direct Dutch BV, Piet Heinplein 1A, 2518 CA Den Haag, The Netherlands. Tel: (070) 365 4677.

Dutch for Foreigners, Postbus 9509, 1006 GA Amsterdam, The Netherlands. Tel: (020) 610 1230.

Elsevier Talen, Van de Sande Bakhuyzenstraat 4 IV, 1061 AG Amsterdam, The Netherlands. Tel: (020) 515 9290. Fax: (020) 515 9298.

Goethe Institut, Herengracht 470, 1017 CA Amsterdam, The Netherlands. Tel: (020) 623 0421. Fax: (020) 638 4631.

Instituut voor Talen, Gebouw Aurora, Stadhouderskade 2, 1054 ES Amsterdam, The Netherlands. Tel: (020) 685 2991. Fax: (020) 685 2681.

ITHA-Dutch Language Courses, Mathenesserlaan 253, 3021 HD Rotterdam, The Netherlands. Tel: (010) 425 4579. Fax: (010) 244 7031.

James Boswell Instituut, Universiteit Utrecht, Bijlhouwerstraat 6, 3511 ZC Utrecht, The Netherlands. Tel: (030) 253 8666. Fax: (030) 253 8686.

Linguaphone, Carlton Place, 111 Upper Richmond Road, London SW15 2TJ, UK. Tel: (020) 8333 4852. Fax: (020) 8333 4897.

NUFFIC (Netherlands Organisation for Cooperation in Higher Education), Postbus 29777, 2502 LT Den Haag, The Netherlands. Tel: (070) 426 0141. Fax: (070) 426 0149.

Studiecentrum Talen Eindhoven B.V., Heggeranklaan 1, 5643 BP Eindhoven, The Netherlands. Tel: (040) 245 2860. Fax: (040) 246 0455.

University of Westminster, School of Languages, 9-18 Euston Centre, London NW1 3ET, UK. Tel: (020) 7911 5000 ext 4355.

Volksuniversiteit Amsterdam, Rapenburgerstraat 73, 1011 VK Amsterdam, The Netherlands. Tel: (020) 626 1626.

Vrije Universiteit, Taalcentrum, De Boelelaan 1105, Room 9A 42, 1081 HV Amsterdam, The Netherlands. Tel: (020) 444 6420.

RECRUITMENT AGENCIES

Algemene Bond Uitzendondernemingen (ABU), Postbus 302, 1170 AH Badhoevedorp, Amsterdam, The Netherlands. Tel: (020) 658 0101.

BBB Uitzendorganisatie, Head Office, Postbus 642, 1180 AP Amstelveen, The Netherlands. Tel: (020) 347 1047. Fax: (020) 645 4853.

Holland Uitzendbureau, Postbus 15717, 1001 NE Amsterdam, The Netherlands. Tel: (020) 639 3059. Fax: (020) 639 2541.

Job-In Uitzendbureau, Javastraat 35a, 2585 AD Den Haag, The Netherlands. Tel: (070) 363 5120. Fax: (070) 363 3851.

KELLY Services, Postbus 3220, 3502 GE Utrecht, The Netherlands. Tel: (030) 280 6600. Fax: (030) 280 6650.

Manpower Uitzendorganisatie, Head Office, Postbus 12150, 1100 AD Amsterdam, The Netherlands. Tel: (020) 660 2222. Fax: (020) 600 2136.

Randstad Uitzendbureau, Head Office, Postbus 12600, 1100 AP Amsterdam, The Netherlands. Tel: (020) 569 5911. Fax: (020) 569 5520.

Tempo-Team Uitzendbureau, Head Office, Postbus 12700, 1100 AS Amsterdam, The Netherlands. Tel: (020) 569 5922. Fax: (020) 569 5243.

Unique Uitzendbureau, Head Office, Postbus 1, 1300 AA Almere, The Netherlands. Tel: (036) 538 2400. Fax: (036) 538 2401.

MISCELLANEOUS ADDRESSES (THE NETHERLANDS)

ACCESS, Plein 24, 2511 CS Den Haag, The Netherlands. Tel: (070) 346 2525. Fax: (070) 356 1332.

Belastingdienst/Centraal Bureau Motorrijtuigenbelasting (Central Motor Tax Office), Postbus 9047, 7300 GJ Apeldoorn, The Netherlands. Tel: (055) 578 2244.

Belastingdienst/Directie douane (Customs Directorate), Postbus 50964, 3007 CA Rotterdam, The Netherlands. Tel: (010) 290 4949.

Centraal Bureau voor de Arbeidsvoorziening (Employment Service), Postbus 5814, 2280 AK Rijswijk, The Netherlands. Tel: (070) 313 0911.

Centraal Orgaan van de Landelijke Opleidingsorganen (COLO), Postbus 7259, 2701 AG Zoetermeer, The Netherlands. Tel: (079) 352 3000. Fax: (079) 351 5478.

Koninklijke Algemeene Vereeniging voor Bloembollencultuur (KAVB), Postbus 175, 2180 AD Hillegom, The Netherlands. Tel: (0252) 515 254. Fax: (0252) 519 714.

Ministerie van Financiën, Central Information Directorate, Postbus 20201, 2500 EE Den Haag, The Netherlands. Tel: (070) 342 7542.

Ministerie van Justitie, Immigration and Naturalization Service, Postbus 30125, 2500 GC Den Haag, The Netherlands. Tel: (070) 370 3124/3144. Fax: (070) 370 3134.

Ministerie van Sociale Zaken en Werkgelegenheid, Directie Voorlichting, Postbus 90801, 2509 LV Den Haag, The Netherlands.

De Nederlandse Organisatie Vrijwilligerswerk, Information and Documentation Department, Postbus 2877, 3500 GW Utrecht, The Netherlands. Tel: (030) 231 9844.

Nederlandse Vereniging van Makelaars o.g. en vastgoeddeskundigen

NVM, Postbus 2222, 3430 DC Nieuwegein, The Netherlands. Tel: (030) 608 5185. Fax: (030) 608 5185.

Netherlands Foreign Investment Agency, Postbus 20101, 2500 EC Den Haag, The Netherlands. Tel: (070) 379 8911. Fax: (070) 347 4081.

NUFFIC, Postbus 29777, 2502 LT Den Haag, The Netherlands. Tel: (070) 426 0260. Fax: (070) 426 0399.

Rijksdienst voor het Wegverkeer (National Vehicle Administration Agency), Skager Rak 10, 9642 CZ Veendam, The Netherlands. Tel: (0598) 624 240.

Syntens, Koninginnegracht 61–62, 2514 AE Den Haag, The Netherlands. Tel: (070) 356 7676.

MISCELLANEOUS ADDRESSES (UK)

Benefits Agency, Pensions and Overseas Benefits Directorate, Department of Social Security, Tyneview Park, Benton, Newcastle upon Tyne NE98 1BA, UK. Tel: (0191) 218 7777. Fax: (0191) 218 7293.

British Association of Removers, 3 Churchill Court, 58 Station Road, North Harrow HA2 7SA, UK. Tel: (020) 8861 3331. Fax: (020) 8861 3332.

The Contributions Agency, International Services, Department of Social Security, Longbenton, Newcastle upon Tyne NE98 1YX, UK. Tel: (0191) 225 4811. Fax: (0191) 225 7800.

DTI Publications Orderline, ADMAIL 528, London SW1W 8YT, UK. Tel: (0870) 1502 500. Fax: (0870) 1502 100.

Institute of Personnel and Development, Publishing Department, IPD House, 35 Camp Road, London SW19 4UX, UK. Tel: (020) 8971 9000. Fax: (020) 8263 3333.

The Legalisation Office, Foreign and Commonwealth Office, 20 Victoria Street, London SW1H 0NZ, UK. Tel: (020) 7210 2521.

Ministry of Agriculture, Fisheries and Food, 1a Page Street, London SW1P 4PQ, UK. Tel: (0870) 241 1710.

NARIC, Ecctis 2000 Ltd, Oriel House, Oriel Road, Cheltenham, Gloucestershire GL50 1XP, UK. Tel: (01242) 260010.

Netherlands British Chamber of Commerce, The Dutch House, 307-308 High Holborn, London WC1V 7LS, UK. Tel: (020) 7405 1358. Fax: (020) 7405 1689.

Glossary

Acceptgiro. Form used to make payment of bills easier. The payee's account details and often the amount and your own account details will be pre-printed.

Alarm nummer. The emergency police/fire/ambulance number 112.

Bedrag (in letters). Amount (in words).

Betaalautomaten. Automatic machines used for 'pinnen' (see below).

Bevolkingsregister. Population register. Every resident must register with the local Population Register. Each time you move, you must visit the Town Hall to remove the old registration and re-register with your new address.

Borrel. Drink (alcoholic).

Borreluur. Cocktail hour.

Chipper/Chipknip. 'Electronic purse' incorporated into bankcard, *Europas* or *Giropas*, which can be used to pay small amounts in many shops.

Er zijn nog twee/drie/tien wachtenden voor u. There are two/three/ten people in front of you (used with telephone queuing systems).

Gemeente. Municipality.

Gewestelijke Arbeidsbureau. Employment office.

Girorekening. Postbank giro account.

Hagelslag. Various kinds of sweet strands or flakes eaten on bread, crispbreads, rusks *etc*, especially at breakfast.

Handtekening. Signature.

Hartelijk gefeliciteerd. Congratulations – also used instead of happy birthday.

HAVO. Senior general secondary education.

Kamer van Koophandel. Chamber of Commerce.

Koffiemelk. Thick evaporated milk, used in coffee.

Koninginnedag. The Queen's official birthday.

Koopavond. Late-night opening for shops.

Kraamzorgverenigingen. Home maternity services which can provide assistance for eight days after the birth; you must register by the end of the third month of pregnancy.

Leerlingwezen. Apprenticeships.

Makelaar. Estate agent.

Onroerendgoedbelasting. Property tax, which must be paid on any property owned or used by you; if you own the property you live in, you pay both as owner and user.

Overschrijvingsformulieren/overschrijvingskaarten. Forms used to transfer money from your bank/giro account directly into another account.

Pinnen. Using a debit card together with a PIN number to pay in shops, garages, restaurants *etc* which have automatic machines.

SOFI nummer. Fiscal social number – your tax and social security reference number, which you must have before you start work.

Stad-streek abonnement. Bus, tram and metro season ticket that can be bought in conjunction with a train season ticket.

Strippenkaart. Bus, tram and metro ticket made up of individual strips, which can be used all over the country.

Te Huur Aangeboden. To rent.

Terwerkstellingsvergunning. Work permit.

Treintaxi. Taxis operating at over 100 stations, offering rail passengers flat-price fares within a certain area.

Uitzendbureau. Agency offering temporary work.

Verblijfsvergunning. Residence permit.

VMBO. Pre-vocational secondary education.

Vreemdelingenpolitie. Aliens Police, with whom you must register if you are planning to stay in the country, and to whom you must apply for a residence permit.

VWO. Pre-university education.

Winterschotels. Dutch winter dishes.

Woonvergunning. Housing permit. Needed to rent or buy many houses and flats.

Ziekenfonds. State-controlled health insurance fund; in most cases, you will automatically be insured with such a fund through your employer if your income is below a certain level.

Further Reading

PERIODICALS

Expat at Home, Postbus 17427, 1001 JK Amsterdam, The Netherlands. Tel: (020) 620 8517.

DTI Publications Orderline, ADMAIL 528, London SW1W 8YT, UK. Tel: (0870) 1502 500. Fax: (0870) 1502 100.

Overseas Jobs Express, Premier House, Shoreham Airport, Sussex BN43 5FF, UK. Tel: (01273) 440220. Fax: (01273) 440229.

Roundabout, Postbus 96813, 2509 JE Den Haag, The Netherlands. Tel: (070) 324 1611.

BOOKS

AA Beadeker's Netherlands (AA Publishing).

Amsterdam: The Rough Guide, Martin Dunford and Jack Holland (Rough Guides).

The Art of Dutch Cooking, C. Countess van Limburg Stirum (Hippocrene Books, Inc.).

At Home in Holland (American Women's Club of The Hague).

Blue Guide: Amsterdam, Charles Ford (A&C Black).

DK Travel Guide: Amsterdam (Dorling Kindersley).

The Flavours of Holland, Hilary Keatinge and Anneke Peters (Schuyt & Co).

Fodor's The Netherlands, Belgium, Luxembourg (Fodor).

Here's Holland, Sheila Gazalah-Weevers (Sheila Gazalah-Weevers).

The Holland Handbook, NUFFIC (X-Pat Media).

Holland: The Rough Guide, Martin Dunford, Phil Lee and Jack Holland (Rough Guides).

Inside Information, Caroline Gelderman.

Live and Work in Belgium, The Netherlands & Luxembourg, André de Vries (Vacation Work).

The Low Sky, Han van der Horst (Scriptum NUFFIC).

The 'Time Out Guide' to Amsterdam (Penguin Books).

The Undutchables, Colin White and Laurie Boucke (White Boucke Publishing).

BOOKLETS AND LEAFLETS

Access Calendar, ACCESS, Plein 24, 2511 CS Den Haag, The Netherlands. Tel: (070) 346 2525. Fax: (070) 356 1332.

The Admission of EU/EAA Nationals to the Netherlands, Ministerie van Justitie, Immigration and Naturalization Service, Postbus 30125, 2500 GC Den Haag, The Netherlands. Tel: (070) 370 3124/3144. Fax: (070) 370 3134.

Contracts and Terms and Conditions of Employment (European Management Guides series), Institute of Personnel and Development, Publishing Department, IPD House, 35 Camp Road, London SW19 4UX, UK. Tel: (020) 8971 9000. Fax: (020) 8263 3333.

Education in the Netherlands, Ministry of Education, Culture and Science, Postbus 25000, 2700 LZ Zoetermeer, The Netherlands. Tel: (079) 323 4854. Fax: (079) 323 2089.

Europe Open for Professionals, DTI Publications Orderline, ADMAIL 528, London SW1W 8YT, UK. Tel: (0870) 1502 500. Fax: (0870) 1502 100.

General Information Guide for American Citizens Residing in the Netherlands, American Consulate General, Museumplein 19, 1071 DJ Amsterdam, The Netherlands. Tel: (020) 575 5309.

Going Abroad and Social Security Benefits, The Benefits Agency, Pensions and Overseas Benefits Directorate, Department of Social Security, Tyneview Park, Benton, Newcastle upon Tyne, NE98 1BA, UK. Tel: (0191) 218 7777. Fax: (0191) 218 7293.

Going to School in the Netherlands, DOP, Postbus 20014, 2500 AN Den Haag, The Netherlands.

Health Care in The Netherlands, ACCESS, Plein 24, 2511 CS Den Haag, The Netherlands. Tel: (070) 346 2525. Fax: (070) 356 1332.

The Job Booklet, ACCESS, Plein 24, 2511 CS Den Haag, The Netherlands. Tel: (070) 346 2525. Fax: (070) 356 1332.

Living and Working in the Netherlands, British Embassy, Lange Voorhout 10, 2514 ED Den Haag, The Netherlands. Tel: (070) 427 0427.

Moving to the Netherlands, Tax and Customs Administration, Customs Directorate (Directie Douane), Postbus 50964, 3007 BG Rotterdam, The Netherlands. Tel. (010) 290 4949.

Netherlands Foreign Investment Agency Information Manual, Netherlands Foreign Investment Agency, Postbus 20101, 2500 EC Den Haag, The Netherlands. Tel: (070) 379 8911. Fax: (070) 347 4081.

Non-university Dutch language courses in the Netherlands, Foreign

Student Service, Oranje Nassaulaan 5, 1075 AH Amsterdam, The Netherlands. Tel: (020) 671 5915.

Residents and non-Residents (IR20), PO Box 37, St Austell, Cornwall PL25 5YN, UK. Tel: (0845) 9000404.

A short survey of social security in the Netherlands, Ministerie van Sociale Zaken en Werkgelegenheid, Directie Voorlichting, Postbus 90801, 2509 LV Den Haag, The Netherlands.

Taxation in the Netherlands, Ministry of Finance, Central Information Directorate, Postbus 20201, 2500 EE Den Haag, The Netherlands. Tel: (070) 342 7542.

You and your NVM-broker, Nederlandse Vereniging van Makelaars in o.g. en vastgoeddeskundigen NVM, Postbus 2222, 3430 DC Nieuwegein, The Netherlands. Tel: (030) 608 5185. Fax: (030) 603 4003.

Your car or motorcycle and the registration papers, Rijksdienst voor het Wegverkeer, Skager Rak 10, 9642 CZ Veendam, The Netherlands. Tel: (0598) 62 42 40.

Your Social Security Rights When Moving Within The European Union, The Stationery Office (Agency section), 51 Nine Elms Lane, London SW8 5DR, UK. Tel: (020) 7873 9090. Fax: (020) 7873 8463.

Your social security insurance, benefits and health care rights in the European Community, and in Iceland, Liechtenstein and Norway, The Benefits Agency, Pensions and Overseas Benefits Directorate, Department of Social Security, Tyneview Park, Benton, Newcastle upon Tyne, NE98 1BA, UK. Tel: (0191) 218 7777. Fax (0191) 218 7293.

Index